REMINISCES OF AN OLD MAN

REMINISCES
OF AN OLD MAN

DENNIS ESLER

Copyright © 2012 by Dennis Esler.

Library of Congress Control Number: 2012914159
ISBN: Softcover   978-1-4771-5537-0
             Ebook   978-1-4771-5538-7

All rights reserved. No part of this book may be reproduced or transmitted in any form or by any means, electronic or mechanical, including photocopying, recording, or by any information storage and retrieval system, without permission in writing from the copyright owner.

This book was printed in the United States of America.

To order additional copies of this book, contact:
Xlibris Corporation
1-888-795-4274
www.Xlibris.com
Orders@Xlibris.com
120767

This is a book of prose and poetry that has been written over the years of my life. Some will find my life exciting, and others will find it to be very boring. So be it.

I was born in one of the suburbs of Minneapolis, Minnesota but by the time I was six years old I knew that life in the metropolis was not for me. I wanted my life to be freer and relaxed than what the metro area could ever provide. We were dirt poor at the time and it affected many of the decisions that I and my family had to make over the years. My brothers and sisters were happy living there but I was not. I put up with this life as long as I could but by the time I was ten I knew I had to get out of the rat race. I had an uncle that lived in Northeastern Minnesota. He was widowed and lived alone with his son. I begged and pleaded until my father finally agreed that I could go there and live.

Before this had happened our family lived thru some very tough times but for now that is another story. In total I attended thirteen schools before finally graduating in 1957 at Biwabik, Minnesota as a nineteen year old. I began writing poetry while in the tenth grade, and some of them will be included in this book. Some of these poems also have appeared in other books that I have written.

CHAPTER ONE

My father and mother each were from a family of seven brothers and sisters so it is not surprising that we had six in our family. I was the youngest of the six and the family brat. My father was working for the Minneapolis news paper at the time and had a full time job. The biggest reason for our financial difficulties was two fold. Dad was a drinker and gambler. There were many weeks that there was no paycheck by the time he got home because he had played poker with his fellow workers and lost. When I was three years old we lived in an apartment in south Minneapolis. The rent was due and Dad had no money to pay. He borrowed a car from one on his fellow workers and told my Mother to round up all of us kids because we were going for a ride. We were riding northwest of the city when we found an abandoned farm near Buffalo, Minnesota. Dad turned into the driveway and asked Mother if she thought it would work. She replied that she wanted to look it over. We got out of the car and went to look at the house. It was not locked so we walked right in. It was not in bad shape so Mom said it would be alright. They unloaded us kids and Dad got back in the car and drove away. We would see him twice in the next five months.

Peggy, my oldest sister was sixteen at the time. Duane my oldest brother was fourteen. Then came two sisters, Vivian, twelve and Elaine was eleven. David was eight and I was the caboose at three. This may not sound like much of a crew to accomplish all the work that had to be done before we could live like most people, but we did it.

The yard was so grown up in weeds that were taller than my mother and the place was over run with several different kinds of snakes. The house and yard were bordering a lake that provided a great surplus of frogs and toads. Little did we know at the time that they would be our main source of food.

Mother had brought along some of our clothes and a few dishes and pots and pans. She also had a small amount of staples such as flour and sugar and salt and pepper. She also knew that there would not be any more when these things were gone.

She told the older children to check over the farm to see if there were any tools or anything else that was useful. They scattered around the yard and found several things. The people that had abandoned the place had left several hoes, rakes, shovels, hammers, an axe and so forth. They would all be put to use before long. We had no idea who owned the farm, or if they would protest our being there but when you have nothing, that is the way you hold body and soul together.

The next morning Mother gave everyone of us a tool of some kind. She then told us that all of the weeds in the yards were German soldiers and that it was our job to help win the war that had just begun. We were to go out and kill as many "German soldiers" as possible. We were to clear the entire yard before supper time that night. Duane and David immediately decided that they would have more fun doing the job if they did it their way. They began to make paths thru the weeds that went everywhere around the yard. They then named them as streets and called the rest of us together so they could explain what they were doing. They even named one of the streets "Dennie" street. I was so proud to have a street named for me.

After Mom seen what the boys had done she decided that all of the yard didn't have to be cleared She did have us clear a spot for a garden as she had found some old seeds in the house. We cleared a spot for a garden and Mother and Duane used the spade to dig a small garden and plant it with the seeds she had found. About this time a car arrived in the yard. We were happy to see that it was aunt Rosie, Dads youngest sister, and uncle Lloyd. They also were having a tough time so they brought their two children Nancy, who was five, and Joe who was two. They asked my mother if she thought she could handle two more children on her farm. She said yes, so they left the children there with us.

Like I said the place was over run with frogs and snakes but they were both a blessing and a curse. The frogs eventually would be our main source of meat, but the snakes were something that Mother could not abide. We killed every snake that we could. I know a lot of you will think that this was wrong, but at the time no one seemed to know any better. The surrounding fields were all farmed to raise field corn for sale. Mother told us that it was just as good to eat as any other so we picked and ate all we wanted.

My sister Peggy got married to a kid by the name of Chet. They moved into a little shed at the back of the same farm.

Joe was to become my friend and confidante and still is yet today. You will see throughout the book where we have done everything together.

At Buffalo

When I was really very small
We stayed out on a farm,
To live thru our depression
And to keep us safe from harm.

It wasn't safe as you may think,
Life was a hazard there.
There really was no heat or lights,
And the cupboards were most bare.

My mother though, did care for us,
While Father worked away.
My sisters and my brothers,
Walked to school every day.

Of sisters, I had plenty,
They numbered up to three,
Of brothers two, and cousins,
That lived along with me.

An old abandoned farmstead
That was over run with weeds,
And the shoreline of a swampy lake
That provided for our needs.

We'd sometimes take a bath there,
If bloodsuckers weren't too thick,
We'd scrape them off when we came out
With the use of a stick.

We'd often walk along the shore
To catch some big bullfrogs,
One time we had a pheasant
That was caught by our big dog.

We would wander in the neighbor's fields
To pick some field corn
Then we'd grind it up and mix it
For pancakes the next morn.

We lived on field corn and frogs
And made our lives go on
And one time got some vegetables,
From the neighbors cross the pond.

My oldest sister Peggy,
And her husband, name of Chet,
Lived in a little shanty,
And they were worse off yet.

Their yard was over run with weeds
As I have said before,
And their house stood on a nest of snakes
That would come up thru the floor.

They killed so many snakes there,
You just really won't believe,
That there was no remorse then,
Cause they had no time to grieve.

The snakes just came from everywhere,
But Mother quickly drew
A battle plan to thin them out,
She hit them with her shoe.

First we thinned the weeds out.
We called them "German Krauts."
Then we planted garden,
Which gave up darn few sprouts.

Next we carved out pathways
To the places where we'd go.
And it was cross these pathways,
Where the snakes would always show.

When walking down a pathway
If a snake did show its head
Off came my mother's slipper,
Or someone else's shoe instead.

The shoe would be her weapon
As Mother did go into war.
Those vipers never stood a chance
As Mom evened up the score.

One day with cousin Nancy,
My Mom and I had walked
Out to our little garden where
We all stood there and talked.

Nancy had her shoes on,
Barefoot were Mom and I,
When a snake appeared, and like a flash,
My Mother made her try.

Off from the foot of Nancy
My mother grabbed her shoe
And after stripped viper
The woman quickly flew.

She soon had won her battle,
But another one arose,
Nancy wouldn't put her shoe on,
She cried it was too gross.

To wear a shoe that killed a snake
Was far below her level.
She said bad things about my Mom,
She really was a devil.

Her brother Joe, my lifelong friend,
Was sitting in a swing,
It really was a rope and board,
A temper mental thing.

But as so often happened,
The board had fallen out,
And Joe was sitting on the rope
When we heard his frantic shout.

We all had run so quickly,
Such a noise that kid did make,
We found him with his feet up,
Just screaming at a snake.

"He sticked his tongue out" Joey cried,
To move he would not try.
But then my Mother sent the snake
To a home up in the sky.

No way to tell how many snakes
She sent down that same road,
But I know that if in a pile
They'd make an awful load.

When winter came we moved away
To a place we called "The Diner"
How quick we were to grasp at straws,
Cause it wasn't that much finer.

CHAPTER TWO

The Diner

The diner was just exactly what it sounds like. Just one mile west of Oak Knoll, Minnesota was an old railroad dining car. Someone had bought it and set it on a cement foundation. It may possibly have been a foundation for something else previously as it didn't fit the dining car frame as it should have. The car hung over each end by several feet. Also since the foundation was cut into a hillside the lower edge was wide open to the weather. This allowed the wind to blow directly under the diner and it was never warm in the winter time. Of course the dining car had never been insulated for a Minnesota winter either so it was not the ideal place to live.
As fall approached at the deserted farm near Buffalo, my parents realized that we would not be able to stay there over the winter. Instead of looking for another place to squat my Father went to talk to Rosie and Lloyd. Lloyd would soon be leaving for a job in northern Canada working on the Alaskan Highway. Rosie would be living alone, and had to work, so it was decided that if we moved in with Rosie that my mother could take of Joe as she had done all summer. I think we moved in at the tail end of October. My brothers and sisters and Nancy were in school all day so it was just Joe and I that needed to be taken care of.

This would have worked all right except for one thing, Nancy was a physically run down as the rest of us were. Therefore she caught, and brought home, every illness. Once she arrived home, Joe and I caught it from her. We caught every type of measles, mumps, chicken pox, whooping cough and everything else available. We also surprised the doctors attending us by catching most of them twice. The medical community will try to tell you that you cannot catch them twice—I'm here to tell you that yes you can. Joe and I did and it was verified by doctors every time. I had a very severe rupture at the same time and I was a very sick boy. Joe also was a very sick boy. When he caught the whooping cough he became so sick that when he coughed, he would get such a nosebleed that the blood would squirt clear across the room. Mother tried every remedy that she knew or heard of, but all to no avail. Sometimes he would cough until he passed out. It was all very scary

Be fore I go any farther let me explain one thing. These are not stories that someone told me. I not only have always had a fantastic memory but I have recently surprised my sisters by telling them about the house we lived in before we moved to south Minneapolis. This was sixty seven years in the past. Vivian didn't believe it even then until I sat down and drew a map of the house and told her what color each one of the rooms had been. Aunt Rosie happened to have saved pictures of our house in Crosby, Minnesota, and every room was just as I had said. I do remember each of these episodes.

From the upper side of our yard we could look right past the village of Oak Knoll and see the Minneapolis skyline at night. This of course was during the Second World War and Minneapolis and other large cities as well would occasionally have to practice blackout drills. The sirens would all sound and then the entire city would go black. Next huge searchlights would come on and would rake across the sky as if looking for German war planes. Eventually the lights would return and the exercise was over.

The Diner

We lived in an old dining car
When I was still quite small.
I do remember quite a bit,
But I don't remember all.

A short ways to the west of town,
We still could see the lights,
When darkness came to visit us,
In the time we called the nights.

But sometimes darkness overcame
The city lights as well
When blackout times were practiced then,
As my parents used to tell.

It was the war that caused this darkness,
Though the war was far away.
President Roosevelt said to "practice,"
So we "practiced," as they say.

Then the giant searchlights
Would sweep across the sky,
As though to catch some German planes,
If they were passing by.

Of course there were no Germans,
And Japan was far away.
But it left a lot of memories
That I carry yet today.

Dennis Esler
b. 1938 in the depths of Minnesota's Winter
Local Author/Poet-Free readings upon request

Writings focus on
- The substance of life, death, & nature
- The telling of man and spirit
- The realms of joy and agony

Writings are
- Philosophical
- Humanitarian
- Humorous or Serious
- Gleaned from the wisdom of old people, experiences with man and nature, observations and inner thoughts

Published:	Titles:
2007	"Like Brothers" — Boys growing up
2008	"Tales of a Teenager" — Author's Life Story
2009	"Reminisces of an Old Man" — Poetry
2010	"A Tale of Survival" — Two women's story
2011	"Settlers of Fox Lake" — 1870 fictional account
2014	"Campfires on a Northern Shore" — Mostly true yarns

Contact Dennis   218-638-2298 or denesler@yahoo.com

Janice Graham wrote this up for Dennis, framed it, and gave it to him to display on the table he would set up to sell his books. He liked it!

The war was not the only thing
I remember of this place,
For it was now that I began
To get started in life's race.

I do remember other places
Where we had lived before,
But now things were more clear to me,
I was no longer four.

I was five years old when we moved
Into this dining car
That stood upon a hill
From which you could see far.

Close down below a creek did run
Thru a large cattail swamp,
With pheasants, yes, and wild ducks too
And a backyard that stayed damp.

Behind the house and down below,
The chicken coop did stand.
There lived our big black rooster
And from this one, I ran.

There were of course a lot of hens,
Big white and gentle birds.
Along with reds and oranges too,
Some black hens could be heard.

I loved the hens and called them mine,
Gathered eggs up every day,
But when that rooster came around,
You never saw me stay.

I'd run and cry, as he would
Chase me from the pen.
I'd tell my Mom that I was scared
But she'd send me back again.

Across the major highway
From the diner where we stayed,
There was a grove of sumac trees,
And in this grove we played.

My sisters had a playhouse,
And my brother had a fort,
And in this grove of sumac trees
Was many hours sport.

In winter time we also played
Upon the frozen creek,
Or went sliding on the hillside,
Or we'd play hide and seek.

We never lacked for fun there,
With all the neighbor boys.
But there was one who lived next door
Who often broke my toys.

He was maybe two years older
Than my age at the time,
I often wished that he'd get lost
Out in the swampy slime.

He really was a meanie,
Beat me up most everyday,
But sometimes my big brothers
Would make this bully pay.

His parents were not willing
To correct him for his deeds,
They thought the world against them,
In their life and in their needs.

They were of German origin
And times right then were bad.
The Mother smoked a corncob pipe,
So did this frightful lad.

She thought him "cute" when he was bad,
But he really was a brat.
How many times, I wished in dreams,
That I could knock him flat.

I never did a thorough job
Tho our sizes did compare,
I was a sickly weakling child,
And the drive was just not there.

I played instead with cousin Joe,
Very nearly of my age,
We got along like brothers,
For our lives we set the stage.

Seems we've always been together
Doing things you'll not believe,
We've had some grand adventures,
In the country where we lived.

There even are some stories
In town, when times were hard,
But our hearts were in the country.
That's why he was my pard.

We were good friends as cousins are
And nothing was ever finer
He lived with us and his sister too
When we all lived at "The Diner."

CHAPTER THREE

Before school began the next year we were on the move again. This time we moved even farther west of Minneapolis near the town of Long Lake. This time we moved onto a real working farm and we even paid rent here that amounted to two dollars per month. The fellow that owned the farm was a German but not at all like our neighbors at The Diner. This fellow had no sympathies for his home land and he applauded every advance that the Allies made. He did all of his farm work with the use of horses and he would sometimes stable them over night at the farm. He lived several miles away so he didn't like to take the time, or tire out his horses by taking them down the roads where there was traffic.

August Meyers was as nice an old gentleman as you would ever find. He was always very pleasant with us all but he was especially nice to me. When he was working the horses in the field he would often allow me to ride the horses. He told me the horses names and then he lifted me aboard to play cowboy while they worked. I rode many cowboy miles and never left the farm.

The first year we lived there he had the fields planted in corn. I loved to walk in the corn fields and smell the corn growing. There were a lot of pheasants as there was a large cattail swamp just west of the farm where the pheasants lived. One day my brother David told me that he had heard of a way to get a pheasant to eat. We took a length of fishing line and tied a small hook onto the end. We took the line into the cornfield and tied it onto one of the bigger cornstalks. Then we buried the hook in a kernel of corn. We also shelled off a pile of kernels and placed the baited one on the top of the pile. When we returned the next morning, there was a pheasant waiting for us. David wrung it's neck and we took it home for Mother to cook for our supper. From then on we ate pheasant when ever we wanted one.

The following year Mr. Meyers planted wheat. I didn't like this as well because I had enjoyed the corn so much. When fall came and the threshing crew came to thresh the grain, Mr. Meyers came to the house and told my Mother that he had two piles of straw. The larger pile he wanted to bale for sale. The smaller pile was for us kids to play in. He said would she please explain to us all what he intended to do. She assured him that his wishes would be followed. She took Joe and I aside and gave a very stern warning that we were to stay away from the large pile. (By this time Joe's father had been killed down in Arkansas so Joe was living with us.)

Several days later I came out of the house to hear a lot of shouting and laughter coming from the straw pile. I thought Mr. Meyers had returned to bale the straw. When I arrived I found David and several of his friends playing in the large pile of straw. I asked David if Mom knew he was playing in the straw pile. He asked why I wanted to know. When I explained what she had told Joe and I, The other boys all gathered round to listen. When they heard that Mr. Meyers wanted to bail the straw they decided they better leave and David went with them. As I returned to the house Mother saw me come out of the field. She asked me if I had been in the straw pile, and when I said no, she went to check. The pile showed definite signs that someone had been on the pile. She came back and gave me a licking even though I tried to tell her that it wasn't me. If I had said it was David he would have given me a beating as well.

The farm was surrounded by apple orchards on three sides. One orchard belonged to Mr. Meyers, and the rest belonged to another family that raised apples for a business. In the four plus years that we lived there I ate a lot of apples.

The fourth side of the farm bordered on the Great Northern Railroad tracks. The train passed by about one hundred yards from the house. This was soon enough after the great depression that there still were a few bums and hobo's walking the tracks. Although they sometimes stopped for something to eat they never bothered us in a bad way.

It was at the farm where my Dad began to teach me how to shoot a gun and catch a fish. We all enjoyed eating the pheasants, squirrels, and rabbits that lived on the farm, so we all learned how to hunt and shoot them. They along with the fish we all caught made up a large part of our diet. Mother also raised chickens and rabbits and we had them for supper as well. I shot both my first rabbit and first squirrel at the age of seven.

The Farm At Long Lake

We moved one spring onto a farm,
This one was not a fake.
We raised animals, and chickens too,
And ducks without a lake.

We had apples by the bushel
And rabbits by the ton
And though we all worked very hard
We sure had lots of fun.

We only had the house and barns,
The owner tilled the fields.
We collected all the fallen fruit,
But the orchards were his yield.

That's not to say we didn't taste
Some apples here and there.
I'm sure the owner knew of this,
But he really didn't care.

Next door were more huge orchards,
With apples of all kinds,
We also sampled most of these
But the neighbors didn't mind.

They knew that we would only take
What we needed just to eat.
And when it came to friendly folks
These neighbors were so sweet.

They gave my Mother "picking" work,
And the older kids as well.
Except for cousin Joe and me
They all did pick so well.

Joe and I just picked and ate.
We seldom filled a pail.
But from the apple cores behind
We left an easy trail.

We ate them in the summer,
When they were green as grass,
And late into autumn,
When the colored leaves had passed.

We'd roast them in a fire,
And eat them while still hot,
Or sometimes even late at night.
We tried not to get caught.

My folks had set a limit
Of what we could consume,
So we would hide the apple cores
When we ate them in our room.

Then early the next morning
When breakfast was all done
We'd take the cores out to the pig,
Or to the chickens we would run.

The pig and the chickens
Would never leave a trace,
And back we'd go into the house
With a smile upon our face.

The railroad tracks ran near the house
And here we'd often play.
We had to run and wave
As the trains went by each day.

We often gathered up the hay
That grew along the tracks,
The older kids would haul it home
With ropes upon their backs.

The trains went by the whole day thru,
And on into the night
But when "THE EMPIRE BUILDER" rumbled by,
It was a glorious sight.

A brand new modern diesel,
The first we'd ever seen,
With eighteen modern sleeper cars.
This train would really scream.

At ten o'clock each evening,
And early every morn,
With clocklike regularity
Our day was quickly formed.

It would wake us up each morning.
Put us to sleep each night.
Even in my memories now
I still can see that sight.

There was a roadway crossing
At the end of our long drive,
With a bridge the train went under,
Where often we would strive.

To stand upon this wooden bridge,
As trains rolled down the track.
To feel the way that old bridge shook,
Made shivers down my back.

There was a drainage ditch of sorts
That ran across the land.
To carry extra water
Was the way that it was planned.

There never was much water.
But there were a lot of weeds.
In this so called drainage ditch,
My brother's greatest deed.

We had to cross that drainage ditch
As we went to school each day,
So if a little early,
We would often stop and play.

One day in early autumn,
Some snow fell on the ground
That showed some animal tracks there
When next we came around.

The tracks were from a wild mink,
My brother Dave did say,
He said we'd set a trap there,
After school on that day.

Later on that evening
A trap indeed we set,
Then home to tell the others
Of the mink we knew we'd get.

One morning then soon after
The trap indeed held game.
But we were rather leery,
That things were not the same.

The trap hung down a hole there
Between a couple rocks,
And when my brother pulled it out
We saw what we had caught.

I think it is a Civet Cat
He said. His voice in shock,
I think it is a skunk I said,
But it really mattered not.

Already it was busy
Perfuming up the air.
We were too stunned to run away,
So we just stood right there.

Then some rocks we gathered,
And threw stones till it was dead.
Then we went on to school.
Should have gone back home instead.

When first into the school bus,
The kids all moved away.
They left us in the back alone,
But why they didn't say.

I guess we had an odor.
We couldn't tell right then.
You see we'd lost our sense of smell
Back at the dead skunks den.

The teacher though, had sense of smell,
Her voice was full of wrath,
"Go home," She told my brother,
And take yourself a bath.

They didn't send me home that day,
I've often wondered why.
Perhaps I was too far away,
When that skunk he did let fly.

The kids did say I stunk of course,
And made me play alone.
And Mother made me take a bath,
That evening when I got home.

The farm was such a marvelous place
Where relatives would all come,
And all play games together
Till the setting of the sun.

Then Pa would build a fire
That we'd gather round outside,
Where we would roast some hotdogs.
Marshmallows too we tried.

It was a happy time of life,
Until that fateful day,
When oldest brother Dewey,
Uncle Sam did call away.

They sent him to far off Austria
To finish the great war game.
When home again he was alright,
But things were not the same.

My brother and my sisters,
Too old they quickly grew,
To play the games, and have the fun,
That as children we all knew.

Only cousin Joe and I
Continued to have fun,
And though we were two boys it's true,
We lived our lives as one.

CHAPTER FOUR

After four and a half years we left the farm at Long Lake. The owner had decided that the rent should be raised to eight dollars per month, and Dad said that it was too much. By now he was working at the Ford garage in Wayzata. The owner of the garage had a summer cabin on Lake Minnetonka, and we could rent that for six dollars per month. Duane was in the army, Vivian had gotten married, and Elaine no longer lived at home. David and I and Joe were the only ones left besides my folks. There were only two bedrooms so Dad and Mother took one, David took the other, and Joe and I slept on a single cot on the porch. Our bed was too narrow to allow us to sleep side by side, so we slept head to foot. Which ever one of us woke up first would tickle the feet of the other. Then we would start our day.

There was electricity in the house but no water or bathroom. The bathroom was a little shed out behind the house, and the water came from a community upright pump that stood in the middle of a small field across the street. There were about eight houses all using the same pump. In winter it would freeze solid and the only way to get it to work was to take a large tea kettle of hot water and pour inside to melt the ice. Even then you had to keep pumping steadily to get what water you wanted before it froze again. If you saw your neighbor thawing the pump, you grabbed a pail and ran to get water before the pump froze.

The neighbors that lived in the area were all very well to do and their children thought they were much better than Joe and I. We never played with any of them because we had to fight our way into and out of the games. It wasn't worth it so we began to find other ways to have fun. The lake was about one hundred yards away so we first began to fish, mostly for sunfish, and we found a way to catch the most and larger fish than most anyone else. We would carefully walk along the shore of the lake early in the morning before the wind began to blow. We could then see where the sunfish had their nests where the eggs were hatching. We found that if we put our baited hook directly into the nests, that the attending fish would attempt to pick it up and remove it. As soon as we saw the fish pick up the hook we would set the hook. We caught so many fish that way that Mother refused to cook any more, so we began to give them away. Soon all the neighbors turned us down as well so we gave them to customers from the resort that was near. Even that grew old after a few weeks so we began to explore other things to do. Behind the house was a shallow, swampy part of the lake so we went there to explore. Dad had told us not to go there because it was too dangerous for two boys who didn't know how to swim. We didn't find a lot to do there but we found that the place was crawling with leopard frogs which fish love to eat.

About this time Dad came home with several inner tubes from the ford garage. These he took to the lake along with Joe and I and showed us how to lie on top and paddle around. We thought this was great so we became regulars at the resort. The majority of the clients there were either Jewish folks, or black folks. Neither of the peoples seemed to be very good at rowing a boat in crowded conditions within the marina. For a fee of five cents we would climb onto our inner tubes and pull them out of the marina. Then we'd go into the marina and buy a bottle of pop, or a candy bar. Finally the owners of the resort went to my Dad and told him that we had to stop. Too many people were complaining about all the money we were making. Joe came up with the idea to sell bait to the customers instead. We began to dig and sell worms, and night crawlers, or frogs if they wanted large fish. We built a little stand right in our front yard and continued to make money. Again the resort owners went to Dad to make us stop as we were taking business away from them.

There was nothing else to do so Joe and I began to wander in the woods that were nearby. This was a habit that we got into that continues yet today. We both love the deep woods and as much as home there as in our own living rooms.

Coffee Grounds

We went wading in the "Coffee Grounds."
Cousin Joe and I.
To catch the green spotted Leopard Frog,
We were about to try.

Now catching frogs was always fun,
But today it was not funny,
We had to try to catch a lot.
Some guy had offered money.

A nickel per for large ones,
The fellow had implied,
And three cents for the small ones
If green colored was their hide.

We went there nearly every day,
The journey mattered not.
But not with Fathers blessings,
So we better not get caught.

For "Coffee Grounds" was just a name,
A swamp, where ground did quake,
Because it was a floating bog
In one bay of the lake.

We called it "Coffee Grounds" because
It was a grainy brown.
And if two boys had broken thru,
They surely would have drowned.

We couldn't swim a stroke you see,
We were only nine years old.
But when it came to boys adventures,
We both were mighty bold.

We'd climb upon an inner tube,
And float across the lake.
But if we picked the one that leaked
It was a bad mistake.

We'd sometimes walk to "Coffee Grounds."
But floating was more fun.
Then with a board in hand
We'd pretend it was a gun.

We'd sneak up on those vicious frogs,
And whack them on the head,
Then put them into water
To see if they were dead.

If they kicked about and tried to swim
We'd put them in a pail.
But some we'd hit a bit too hard,
So we threw them off our trail.

We saved a lot more than we lost,
Our touch became most fine.
The ones we saved we always used
When it came to fishing time.

The ones we hit a bit too hard
We would often take
Out with us on our inner tubes
To the middle of the lake.

There we'd feed them to the gulls
That often came around.
I wonder why they never fed
Out on the "Coffee Grounds."

Then one day father asked us
If we had some fishing bait.
We told him we'd go get some,
If he'd just sit down and wait.

With swimming trunks and inner tubes,
We quickly made our way
Out to the dark brown "Coffee Grounds"
In the back end of the bay.

We never checked behind us cause
No one followed there.
To go and catch some bait for Pa
Was quite a big affair.

We knew we'd soon be fishing
At the far end of the lake,
Cause Father had a motor now.
Not long would this trip take.

We had gathered frogs for minutes few,
When a boat did soon appear.
The man looked most familiar
As closer he drew near.

With a willow switch in hand,
We knew or fate was sealed,
And when our little dance was done,
You bet our voices squealed.

It really was not funny,
When Father came upon the scene,
And gave us both a spanking,
Though the man was never mean.

It hurt him more than us, I'm sure,
He did it for our sake.
And then he took us fishing
At the far end of the lake.

Sunfish

We often did go fishing
For the large fish in our lake.
When we used the frogs we'd caught,
A bass we hoped to take.

When fishing for the sunfish
We always did use worms,
And more and more to sunfish,
Our attention we did turn.

The sunfish did their spawning
In nests along the shore.
So with a pole, and hook and line,
A limit was no chore.

A limit of the sunfish,
Why, it was no trick at all.
From the breakup of the ice in spring,
Till the freeze up in the fall.

This soon became a daily task,
One day after another.
We'd catch and clean a whole big batch,
Then we'd take them home to Mother.

Mother smiled when first we did this,
But she quickly changed her thoughts.
When she found out in days to come
How many fish we caught.

My first love was the sunfish,
I pursued it with delight.
At mid day's hottest moments,
Or at the dawns first light.

I'd pursue it in the evening,
Till the stars would dance about.
Then I'd take them home to Mother,
Who would answer with a shout.

Take these to the neighbors,
And give them all away.
Just tell them that we have enough
To last till Christmas day.

Still I fished my heart out,
Caught hundreds every day,
And it kept on getting harder
To give them all away.

I even gave to passersby
Who fished upon the lake.
Even they soon turned me down,
No more sunfish would they take.

I finally caught and threw them back,
But hated all the waste.
So I kept the badly injured ones,
And took them home to taste.

Then Father took my fishing pole
And said to fish no more.
He said to find some other game,
Upon this great lakes shore.

I could only catch the sunfish
One day a week he said.
So I took to digging worms
And selling them instead.

I even earned some money
And I kept it in a pod.
Then I went and spent it,
To buy a fishing rod.

Now I could fish much deeper,
Where the bigger sunfish grew.
But though I fished much harder,
The fish I caught were few.

I seemed to lose the magic touch.
I was not at my best.
I forgot to fish the shallows,
Where the sunfish makes its nest.

I learned to catch the walleye,
The crappie and the bass,
And I've had the goose bumps,
When a northern made a pass.

I learned to catch the other kinds.
But I always had a wish,
To someday journey back
And catch some more sunfish.

CHAPTER FIVE

Moving On

After one winter in the summer cabin, with no insulation, we felt we had to move on. Dad found a farm house for rent outside of Champlin, Minnesota. It was owned by one of the Chicago mobsters but the rent was handled by a farmer across the road. We moved in the spring so that meant changing schools again. I should not have worried as we were not there that long.
The most important part about living there was that there was a large forest of oak and maple trees behind the yard. I and brother Dave immediately started hiking in these woods and found them to be very beautiful. One day while hiking in a new area where we had not been previously we found a natural clearing within the woods. It was only about fifty feet across but we thought it would be a perfect place for a tent. David had become a boy scout when we lived at Long Lake so he had all the camping gear that we would need. Finally on Easter weekend we told our parents that we were going camping. I had slept in the tent with David in our back yard before but this was my first time to actually go camping.

We made up packs on our backs and away we went. We finally found the little clearing again and David began to set up the tent. I was busy gathering fire wood so I paid no attention to his choice of location.

By the time he had the tent set up, I had enough fire wood for a week piled nearby. David decided it was time to build a fire so he could cook our supper. The entire forest floor was still deep in last years leaves but he just went ahead and piled the wood according to the Boy Scout manual and then announced that he would show me how to light a campfire with only using two matches to start the fire. The first match went out from the wind before he ever got it near the "fire". The second match blazed brightly as it lit the sticks on fire. Suddenly David called me to help put out a wildfire that was trying to burn the whole forest to ashes. The leaves caught fire because it hadn't rained for several weeks and with the wind that was blowing the whole woods would certainly have burned. Lucky for us there was a depression near at hand that had standing water so we grabbed our bucket and a pot and began to put the fire out. It had burned a spot about ten feet across but David said that he had planned it that way.

After we had eaten our supper we decided it was time for bed. David was careful to show me to look at the sky before going to bed. There were no stars so he told me it may rain but that we were safe because we had a tent. We had only been sleeping a few hours when a thunder storm woke us. We lay in bed and talked about how sorry we felt for all the animals in the forest that were getting wet while we were safe and dry in our tent. About this time I realized that I was getting wet as the tent was leaking. As I went to sit up I put my hand on the ground and found that there was water running thru the tent. When I complained to David he said that it was nothing to worry about and to go back to sleep. I tried but soon the whole tent collapsed. By now our sleeping bags were soaked and we were lying in the water. We crawled out of the tent and went and sat on a stump until daylight. By daylight we knew that we were done camping for this trip. We loaded up our wet gear and returned home in time for breakfast. The only thing that was said was that Dad asked if camping was fun?

That time was a disaster but I fell in love with the idea and I've continued to go camping up until this very day. I never go camping in the public campgrounds with all of the extra's like electricity. I only camp in the wilderness.

Camping

I've written lines about my home
And other places that I'd roam.
Told of places where I'd go
With Brother Dave or cousin Joe.

I've spoke of places that I've seen,
A wooded forest or a pretty stream.
I'll tell you now as we go forth
What happened when we moved "Up North."

But first a minute let me take
Before I make a big mistake,
To tell of one more farmstead home,
Close to the cities where I did roam.

This was our last deserted farm
Where we did live, but meant no harm,
To neighbor folks who lived around
This place they call Anoka town.

Our stay was short, a month or two,
I know the time really flew.
T'was in the spring, round Easter time
This story that I tell in rhyme.

We lived quite near the river there,
About as close as Mom would dare.
This was the father of all the waters,
As Indians told their sons and daughters.

There really was a half a mile
To waters edge, but in the style,
Of mothers, with their fears and dreams
That was close enough to that big stream.

It flowed right thru the neighbors land
Who had a farm that was most grand.
They had pigs and cows and chickens there,
And horses large beyond compare.

With brother Dave I'd often go
To see this farmyard animal show.
To watch the farmer milk his cows,
And sometimes we could feed the sows.

We went there almost every day
To get our milk, for which we would pay.
Maybe even eggs we'd buy
And take them home for Mom to fry.

The cost was small, so we didn't mind,
We knew that we were treated kind,
By this grand farmer and his clan
Who rented us a chunk of land.

A large oak forest grew out back,
So with our tent and sleeping sack
With brother Dave I did explore,
To find a place to camp outdoor.

An opening there we finally found,
To set the tent up on the ground.
Then placed our sleeping bags inside,
To do things right, we really tried.

The sky by dark was filled with clouds
But we just looked, and laughed out loud.
Said "let it rain, a tent we've got."
We should have picked a higher spot.

The ground upon which our tent sat
Was covered with leaves, not very flat.
We should have known from our tent pole
The tent we'd placed down in a hole.

Around midnight when rain began,
The puddles formed, then quickly ran
Into this hole, where we did camp,
And suddenly we were very damp.

Did I say damp? I should say drenched.
When from the ground the tent was wrenched.
It fell right in on top of us,
But all my brother did was cuss.

We stayed right there till morning light,
It was a most disgusting night.
Soaked we were, from bottom to the top,
And still the rain just wouldn't stop.

Six inches deep the water stood.
Floating about was our fire wood.
But no wood there to start a fire,
By now that was my one desire.

Nothing to do but pack on in
And listen to the laughing din.
When we told Father what we'd done,
He asked if camping was a lot of fun.

We still go camping to this very day,
But now I watch how the ground lays.
We'll cross the lake in my old boat
To make darn sure the tent won't float.

Every one who has a story to tell has to come from a family of one kind or another whether you are adopted or natural sons or daughters. A lot of people don't want admit who their family is but since I've already told about part of my family, I'll expand it to include a few more.

My Father had an uncle named Fred. He was a very uneducated man, but by no means was the man not smart. He was born in 1884 and at that time there were no laws about going to school. He was in the second grade when he decided that he was needed at home on the farm more than he was needed in school. By the time he was thirteen he was known as a fine teamster. He seemed to have a way with horses and could make them work as well as anyone. He then moved to northern Wisconsin where he went to work in the logging camps. As the logging industry moved into Minnesota, he just followed along. All loggers had other jobs as well because logging is predominately seasonal work, and so it was with Fred. He worked at many jobs that did not require the ability to read. Math was basic but he knew carpentry enough that he picked up a lot of math in the jobs he did perform. He also learned the art of story telling as that was the only entertainment the men had in the logging camps. He had the ability to hold a persons interest until the punch line.

Because he was uneducated a lot of people took advantage of his limited abilities. If he owned something that someone else desired, they would frequently find some way to put him into a position where he felt it was to his advantage to sell them the item for almost nothing. The other problem that he had was that he felt if some one left a particular piece of machinery or a cow or whatever for an extended period of time, that ownership became his. I once left my bicycle in his care for a month while I went to work on a farm. When I returned I found that he had sold "his" bicycle to a neighbor. This is a problem that plagued him until he died.

Fred had been one of the people who had taken advantage of the Homestead Act, and had filed on a homestead near Tower, Minnesota. Although he never "proved up" on the homestead he did live there fore almost two years. When the ownership was never documented the State of Minnesota assumed ownership and deeded the land to the Park Service and they created a state park out of it. Many of his neighbors used that as a bad name against him that he had never followed thru on the ownership. He had his personal reasons and I find them valid.

When I came to live with him in 1949 he was a widower for many years already. He lived with his youngest son in an old tumble down tar paper shack. Before the house was built the land underneath was never properly prepared. There was an old tree stump under the kitchen floor that the frost had heaved upward until it penetrated the floor and made a sizeable hole thru the floor. The mice and squirrels could run in and out at will. This attracted weasels and I trapped several right there in the kitchen.

He was a wonderful old man of sixty five before I ever got there and when his son left, he and I lived there alone. He was a fair cook and we always got along just fine. I called him Freddie

Uncle Fred

When first I came to Freddie's place,
And saw the look there on his face,
I knew I'd found another friend,
Who would help to shape and bend,
Me into a woodsman, a pioneer,
To hunt the grouse and deer.
To catch the fish with hook and line,
And to make his life a part of mine.

He was Dad's uncle, this pleasant man,
Who had his life so well in hand.
Already age had touched his face,
But even that was well in place.
For sixty five years had flown by,
(there'd be twenty more before he'd die),
And he had learned life's lessons well,
That's why he had so much to tell.

The man was small, as statures go,
But still he set out quick to show
That size did not a giant make.
No backtalk, would this man take.
I learned right off to hold my tongue,
And listen about when he was young.
He had so many stories to tell
And these he told so very well.

He talked of hunting and of fishing too
From southern Wisconsin, and north up thru
The area where we did live.

This man just had so much to give.
He taught me how to set a trap,
Or in the spring to gather sap
From Maple trees along the river,
To make a bow, and arrows, and quiver

From him I learned to cut a tree
Or gather honey from a wild bee,
To harness horses and make them work,
To pull a load with hardly a jerk.
The right way how to milk a cow,
Or store the hay in the barns haymow.
To treat the animals as if my own,
And to harvest crops from the seeds we'd sown

In mid July, in summers heat
We made the hay for the cows to eat.
We also fed some to the horse,
And rabbits and chickens too, of course.
Then, when the day's hard work was done,
We'd head for the river, to have some fun.
We swam, or fished, or sometimes lay
On the rivers bank, to pass the day.

We walked to the river, to and from,
We both marched to the same drum.
He was different from most other folks.
He told me stories, or sometimes jokes,
Of times when he was just a lad.
To be with him always made me glad.
He told me stories that he held dear.
These were the stories that I liked to hear.

He told about the folks around
Between our house and the nearest town.
How few there were when first he came
To settle down and stake a claim
On land that is now a state park,
And why he left it without a mark.

How he went away and then came back
To settle down in this old shack.

He built his home with tools few
With help of neighbors that he knew.
Built it in the deepest wood,
And living there was mighty good.
He then went out and cleared the land,
To make a field in which he planned,
To plant potatoes in a row,
Or anything else he thought would grow.

He raised his farmyard animals there,
Chased off the wolf, and the bear,
And tried his best to provide for all,
When harvest time came round next fall.
He often picked the berries wild,
He'd done this since he was a child,
These he always cleaned and canned,
For winters food he always planned.

We cut the wood and stacked it high,
Sometimes I thought it would reach the sky.
Some pieces large for night time fires
And others small as we'd require.
And kindling wood to build the blaze,
To heat the house for nights and days,
And still more wood for cooking too,
To fry the bacon, or boil the stew.

With winters coming, life was more loose.
One time I even tried his snoose.
We sat around the fire and talked
With Melvin Peterson, who had walked
In from the road (we were snow bound).
That never stopped Melvin from coming round,
He was our friend from across the way,
Who came to see us, every day.

Other friends would stop in too,
To share a story, or a bottle of brew.
Sometimes they'd stay till break of day
Before they'd journey on their way.
Some would come with a song to sing,
We just never knew just what they'd bring.
Most would come to sit and chat,
We really did a lot of that.

But all too soon there came the day
When I grew up and moved away.
I left this man who lived alone
So I could try the things he'd shown.
School was over, the army called
And from then on my life snowballed,
From ocean east, to ocean west,
I'm glad he prepared me for the test.

Freddie's Stories

I used to live with Uncle Fred, when I was but a boy.
The times we spent together were mostly times of joy.
We'd work and play the whole day thru, and often then at night,
While listening to the radio, with his stories he'd delight.

He'd tell of times so long ago, and things that he had done.
They maybe weren't the gospel, but to hear them was still fun.
And maybe they were tainted with language that was blue,
That never kept this boy of ten from hoping they were true.

He'd tell me of blueberries, that wouldn't fit a pail.
And how he'd try to lift them, but it was to no avail,
So he cut them into pieces, large berries now quite small,
Then pull them home with horses, to make jelly for the fall.

Or maybe, he'd tell me of a wood tick he had seen
That was large as any pony, with a disposition mean.
How he'd fashioned up a harness, and plowed the garden plot,
Then turned it loose, to roam again, when the weather got too hot.

Mosquitos too he talked about, and one day did explain
How one landed at the airport, and they thought it was a plane.
So they filled it full of fuel, and sent it on it's way.
And if it's not run out of fuel, it's still flying yet today.

One cold and winters night, he watched a scene unfold,
And this is what he saw that night, or at least what I was told.

Four rabbits playing in the yard, around my stick horse mount,
And two more running round so fast, that these he could not count.

The there was the foo foo, a most unusual bird,
That always did fly backward, or so I always heard,
Now why it did fly backwards is a mystery to me.
But it kept me looking for it, though this bird I did not see.

I never saw a single one of these of these mysterious things
That crawled about the woodlands, or flew on buzzing wings.
Perhaps I wasn't looking when they happened to pass by.
But I know they had to be there, because Freddie, wouldn't lie.

All though Melvin Peterson is not, and never was a relative I including him here because of the strong influence that he had on the way I lived my life. Technically Melvin was my Fathers best friend but he and I also were best friends in father son relationship. He was a farmer by necessity but he worked part time for the local township as an equipment operator. He also was one of the most accomplished outdoors men I've had the pleasure to know. He was completely at home in the deepest forest, and was completely competent on the water of any lake, including Lake Superior. He had all the equipment needed for extended camping and fishing trips into the wilderness, and he and Dad made many trips before I was of an age where I could go and carry my own weight. Once I got to be a teenager Melvin and I made hundreds of trips hunting and fishing. He taught me more about living in the wilderness than any other person. He was not, and never had been married, so we became his "family".

MELVIN

Melvin was our family friend
Who lived just down the road.
The things we learned from him
Really made a load.

He came at first to "Freddie's place"
While I was living there.
Then as we moved to our own homes
He followed every where.

He showed us where to pick the fruit
That grew in this wild land.
And where to find the "Lady Slipper"
Where the pine trees made their stand.

He taught me how to catch the bass,
That were living in his lake,
And then to put the small ones back.
Only keepers could I take.

He taught me where to find the grouse.
Or how to trail a bear.
To find most any wild thing,
He seemed to know just where.

When it came to working deeds,
He always lent a hand.
To saw the wood, or build the house,
On Melvin, we always planned.

The one thing Melvin did the best,
Some people thought his worst.
He kept up on the local news,
He always knew it first.

If widow brown had had a date,
Or some girl was p.g.
He'd make a special trip to tell
It all to our family.

Of course this shy and quiet man
Had many other friends,
So on the road to spread the news,
Many hours he did spend.

He never meant to cause hard times
For the subject of his tales.
Just something new to talk about
As he traveled down life's trails.

But talk or not, he always knew
He was welcome in our home.
Where he and Dad would sit and chat
About places where they'd roam.

They fast became the best of friends
Who worked to help each other,
Till the work was done, then they would go
Fishing with my Mother.

The three of them made many trips
In the wild forests lands.
They all enjoyed them very much
And said those times were grand.

As fall would come, both he and Dad
Would leave their rods alone,
And take instead their shotguns
To find the grouse's home.

They traveled over forest wide,
To find this chestnut bird.
Then back at home, with birds in hand
Many tales would be heard.

They also kept their senses tuned
To other things that mattered.
By the coming of the snow
They knew where the deer were scattered.

When winter came and froze the lake
Into a giant cake of ice.
They'd go and spear the Northern Pike.
That was a part of life.

Yes, Melvin fished and hunted hard,
And did a good days deed.
At helping out his best of friends
With everything they'd need.

He never dressed up fancy,
He had no one to impress.
He sometimes shaved just once a week,
But he was always at his best.

He seldom fouled the air about
With language that was blue.
But he spoke right out with how he felt
With words that were so true.

I heard him cuss and carry on
About things he felt were wrong.
Only when the things he felt,
Hurt his ideals, which were strong.

To speak about someone oppressed
Or of cruelty to a child,
Were enough indeed, to rouse this man,
To the edge of being wild.

He never did a cruel deed.
Or none that I heard of.
But he did a lot of helping folks
And he did it all with love.

Just like another father to me,
I miss him now he's gone.
I've done my best to give him space,
Here in my own life's song.

I miss this man an awful lot
I think of him each day.
And I still try to be like him
As I journey on my way.

I'll tell you now about my Father. Like I said before, I always called him Pa. It was the easiest, and he seemed to like the handle I gave him. He was a very short man, only five foot two but he was a giant to me, not for his size, but for his deeds. He was honest and trustworthy to all of his friends, and he loved my Mother to the point of adoration.

He spoiled me rotten when I was a child, but still I had to share whatever came along just like my siblings. I don't think he ever treated any of his children badly although we all gave him plenty of reasons. He had some really tough times when first we moved north trying to find a job that suited him and could give year round employment. At that time most employment in this area was strictly seasonal. There were the iron mines but those jobs were given out on a personal friendship basis. If you didn't have a personal friend that was a boss, you didn't have a job.

Pa

While I was there with "Freddie"
Not far way I'd roam.
For it was next to Freddie's land,
Where we finally built our home.

I always called him Pa it seems,
I never called him "Pop."
But if I ranked my parents
I would rank them at the top.

My Pa and I were best of friends
When I was but a lad.
He very seldom called me son,
And I seldom called him Dad

We were closer knit than that,
As friends is what we were,
He made the trail that I followed,
To his age I did defer.

He set the guide lines for my life,
The limits plain as day.
And so his tracks I followed
As I journeyed on my way.

I found he seldom steered me wrong,
As I turned here and there.
He let me make my own mistakes,
But he guided me for fair.

This all worked well until the time
I passed an awkward age.
When I would listen to no one,
Those years were called "teenage."

He suffered thru those terrible years,
But always kept his cool.
He said I'd grow right out of it
Once I got out of school.

There finally came a day in spring
When I left home to go
To get a job, and go to work,
In far off Idaho.

My Pa was sad but had to say,
"A man he has become."
I still had oh so much to learn,
I really was quite dumb.

I worked out there for most a year,
Then came back to my home.
But He knew I'd never stay there
Cause I had the urge to roam.

I stayed and finished school days,
That made my Father proud.
When I finally graduated
He was higher than a cloud.

Of sisters and of brothers
None had gone this far before.
He was so very happy
I got praises all galore.

When I went away to Army,
He wrote me every day.
How I waited for those letters,
To see what he would say.

He always kept me posted
Of my friends from round about,
And how he did while hunting,
He never left a doubt.

Then I finally married
Moved my wife down there with me.
His letters kept on coming
But they were for both to see.

Then when our little girl was born
He took her to his lap
And he would safely hold her
While she took her midday nap.

He also held her brothers,
And set them on his knee.
Sometimes I still can see him
Playing with all three.

My Fathers gone away now,
To his eternal sleep,
But I still have loving memories,
And these I'll always keep.

My Mother was a woman that had grown up in very hard times with a family that considered her a black sheep. They used her as a semi slave and her brothers and sisters, not much better. Her mother had been shot in the arm in an accident so the arm had been removed before my mother was born but somehow it became her problem to compensate for it. She never had the life of a normal girl so she left home at a very young age and married my Dad shortly after. She made do with what she had, which was never much.

She raised six children of her own plus half of the relatives children, then when they were all grown, she cared for all the neighbors children. I have always said that it was because she never grew up herself that young people just gravitated toward her.

She had the ability to make a decent meal out of almost nothing and that normally was what we had to eat at home.

Mother

How many kids did Mother raise?
Well, really, I don't know.
There would be a bunch of them,
If in one place they'd show.

First of all there were us six,
Whose life she did begin.
But there were lots of others,
Whose life she gave a spin.

Next came Nancy Jam, and Joe
And others I recall.
Who lived with us in summertime,
But went back home in fall.

Some did stay for shorter times,
And some stayed quite a while.
And I think you must count Chet, as well,
If counting is your style.

Now count one more for Delmar too,
For the time he spent with us.
His home was just across the way,
But with us, there was no fuss.

Chet and Delmar were married, yes,
To Peggy and Elaine.
But they did a lot of growing up
Under Mothers hand, it's plain.

Though they would often come and go,
They called our house their home.
A place to find a mothers love,
When they got too tired to roam.

So I say yes, she raised them too,
Along with all the rest,
And loved them just like all of us,
If that's part of the test.

She helped to raise with all our help
Her grandkids one by one,
And though they were a load for her,
She said it was all fun.

Then she raised another girl,
Suzy, was her name,
Now you can see why raising kids
Was Mothers claim to fame.

Besides the kids that she did raise
And loved as if her own,
There's been at least a hundred more
That my Mothers love has known

They called her "Grandma Goldie,"
Though no kinship could they bear.
So she gave them all the love she could,
And treated them all fair.

From fair haired little boys and girls
To some who'll never learn,
She gave her love and guidance
And asked nothing in return.

That's why I say, I just don't know,
How many counted her as mother.
I counted here as best I could
But I'm sure there have been others.

CHAPTER SIX

As fall approached in 1955 cousin Joe and I began to pay more attention to our surroundings. It seemed that as each day went by that Mother and Dad had more and more work for us to do. There fore we decided it was time for a change. Even though the land we lived on was really mine. Dad decided to give a chunk of it to my sister Vivian.

In 1951 I had been hit by a car in Virginia, Minnesota. When I finally received my huge settlement of $280, people asked what I was going to do with the money. I had made up my mind that my Father had never owned anything in his life. He had dreamed all of my life to be able to own forty acres. So I bought the forty acre plot next to Uncle Fred's land for my parents to live on. We did not have money enough to buy the materials for a house until the summer of 1954. Dad had worked for Melvin Peterson and saved enough money to buy the materials for a 12 foot by 16 foot house. In August he and Joe and I with the help of Melvin and Freddie put up the house. It was only one room but by God it was ours and it was paid for in cash.

Also in 1954 Vivian brought here husband here from Milwaukee, Wisconsin. He knew nothing of living in the north woods, but he was an automotive mechanic so he was able to get a job in a new iron mine that was just opening. He insisted that he and Vivian would build a house of their own if Dad would give them some land, so Dad did. The house that they built was a laugher. Instead of buying cured lumber he went into the woods and cut young green living trees. He flattened two sides and nailed them together. He built the house eight feet wide and thirty feet long. There was just more trees cut to length for a floor. The only lumber used were the boards to build the door frame and the window wells. The windows were ones that a friend of his had taken out of a chicken coop. They lived in the house for one winter and then moved out and rented an abandoned farm house.

In the fall of 1955 Joe and I decided that we could live there if we were allowed to take meals at home, and if Mother would continue to do our laundry. They agreed that we could try it. The shack was clear at the back of the forty so there was no water or electricity. Mother gave us one of her kerosene lamps for light but we had to buy our own kerosene. The wood stove that Vivian had left there would be our heat. We thought we had it made. We had to walk down to the folks house for breakfast and then catch the school bus there.

As January arrived the very cold temperatures arrived as well. One night it was thirty eight degrees below zero when Joe and I got ready for bed. Joe loaded the stove with some coal he had bought, and we went to sleep. About 1:OO'clock something woke me and I immediately realized that the house was on fire. I tried to get Joe out of bed but he was sleeping too soundly and would not wake up. I gave up and ran outside and found the roof all ablaze. There was noting there to throw snow with except the box that the coal had been in. I grabbed the box and began to throw snow. Once I got the fire knocked down enough to leave for a minute, I hurried back inside to try to get Joe to wake up. After I dragged him out of bed he woke up a little when he hit the floor. He wanted to know why I was dressed, and why was there snow on the floor? I told him the house was on fire and he better get out. He walked over and looked into the stove then told me the fire was fine. I had to drag him outside before he got enough awake to function. We went back outside to find the roof blazing again. We thru more snow until we got the fire out, then walked down to the folks to let them know we were alright.

We explained what had happened and Dad said to go to sleep on the couch. I told Joe I better take one more check on our shack. When I got close I could see it was in full blaze again. This time I threw enough to put the fire out for good. There was a five foot hole burned completely thru the roof.

We continued to live in that shack until spring but never did fix the roof. When it would snow the snow would pile on the bed but it was so cold in there that we just shook the blankets and it would all fall off.

The Shack

I'll tell you now of things we done.
Of our good times, and the songs we sung.
How we did travel through our teen years
With a million smiles, and a few tears.

Along about nineteen fifty four
We built our house that was little more
Than four short walls, and a roof above.
But a house we all did build with love.

It wasn't large, that is a fact,
But it was warm, when the wood we stacked
Into the stove that stood alone
Near the eastern wall of our little home.

We cut the wood with a circle saw
On warmer days when the snow did thaw.
On colder days when it would storm.
We'd stay inside where it was warm.

We had a Fordson tractor then
To haul the wood from the forest glen.
We really made my father smile
As larger, larger grew the pile.

When Mom and Pop too stringent grew
We took our things, and quickly flew
To our own place, an abandoned shack
Still on our land, but way out back.

Smaller still this shack of ours,
But in this shack many happy hours.
We often had no warming fire,
But to live alone was our one desire.

We did survive the winters cold
By spending time neath the blankets fold.
Though it was cold, and times were rough,
We got along cause we were tough.

Then came the time, Joe got a check
From the government I do suspect,
So we did buy a load of coal.
To keep us warm was our biggest goal.

We gathered wood in the short daylight,
And only burned the coal at night.
We were in school the whole day thru,
So times to gather wood were few.

One night while we were burning coal,
In the roof above we burned a hole.
About five feet in diameter,
This almost did us in for sure.

Still we stayed in that little shack.
Until spring time, when we moved back,
To live again in my Fathers home.
But we seldom stayed, cause we liked to roam.

He just never knew where we went,
He only knew how much time we spent,
Out in the woods, or on some lake,
Where grouse we'd shoot or fish we'd take.

It was a happy carefree time,
For Joe and me it was so fine.
I'd love to live those days again,
But they are gone like a passing train.

During this same winter Joe and I ran a trap line approximately five miles in length. We were trying to catch what ever was available, but we centered our greatest efforts on mink and weasels. As soon as there was freezing weather we began laying out our line but we didn't get real serious until we had snow enough to run the line on ski's. we started behind our house and went one half a mile to the river, crossed that and proceeded north for a quarter mile or so then made a loop to the west until we finally ran back into the river. Once again we'd cross the river, and head west. There was a several acre stand of pine in that area with several hills. From there it was south thru a huge spruce and muskeg swamp for over a mile to where we turned back north and finally back home. It normally would take between an hour and a half and two hours to complete the run. Of course there were times when it took much longer if we had to move traps to a different location. We never got rich off of our catch but it was spending money for things we wanted. There are no people in this area even yet today. It is a road less area and our line was miles from the nearest house or road.

There came a time when we suddenly were coming up empty and catching nothing. We immediately thought someone else was tending our traps and stealing what we caught.
This brought about this story, which happened just as I tell it here.

A Light In The Night

As a happy young man, still in my teens,
My way of life was the outdoor scene.
Often with others, sometimes alone,
Thru the woods and fields I'd happily roam.

I was often drawn to the river out back,
Or down the road to an old bachelors shack.
To a rundown old farm, or a quiet wood land pond,
I'd explore and enjoy, this far and beyond.

From the gray of the morning, to the dark of the night,
I would seek and enjoy each marvelous sight.
But sometimes those sights were a mystery to me,
Like "The Light in the Night" that once I did see.

With falls turning colors, and winters pure white,
The sign of a mink was a trappers delight.
And these I did seek, for at trapping I tried,
In the creeks and the rivers, and the woods alongside.

Now my hours spent in school used up the daylight
So my trap lines were run in the darkness of night.
The moon, and the stars, were the only light used,
Cause the glare of a flashlight only confused.

With my cousin Joe, I'd ski along our track
And check all our "sets" on our trap line out back.
The night air was cold, often thirty below,
But we'd hurry along with miles still to go.

No roads were we near, they were miles away,
For this is the wilderness where we did play.
No houses at all with their people and lights,
To spoil the beauty of a cold winters night.

Then there came a time when our traps were all bare,
And we caught not the animals that were living there.
We finally arrived at the discouraging thought
That someone was stealing the furs that we caught.

So we skied out more often at odd times of night,
To catch this fur thief, before he slipped out of sight.
Though we tried every trick, and hatched many a plan,
No one could we catch with our fur in his hand.

Then late one dark night on a ridge by the creek,
We spotted the light of the one we did seek.
We quickly agreed we would now catch our man,
We would run and surround him, that was our plan.

With ski's that were flying we covered the ground,
And shortened the distance to the light we had found.
But while still yards away the light suddenly went out,
And we slid to a stop, thinking we had been found out.

We stood oh so quiet in the darkness of night
But no more did appear the "The Light in the Night"
We moved to the spot where the light last had been,
And found to our shock, we were alone once again.

Joe stopped and cried out, "we've been chasing thin air,
We're chasing some one who's not even there."
It had snowed hard that day but no tracks in the snow
To show which way someone would have to go.

I looked and I saw what he said was all true.
The snow was unbroken and no trail showed thru.
The light we had seen is a mystery to me,
But a "Light in the Night" I know we did see.

CHAPTER SEVEN

After I had graduated I went to work for the local railroad. This was a seasonal job so I would work all summer, and draw unemployment each winter. I did a lot of winter fishing with friends or alone. Then in the evenings several friends and I would go to town and terrorize the young ladies that gathered there. We did a lot of dating but like most of the young people of northern climes, we did a lot of drinking as well. There are thousands of stories that could be told but that would make the book X rated then, so they will have to wait. The railroad was tied directly to the mining operations in the area, so if there happened to be a poor demand for iron ore, or if the miners were on strike, we were laid off until things improved. This gave me time for a lot of camping and fishing and I took advantage of every moment. Most of the very enjoyable trips were with Melvin Peterson, or with my cousin Joe. After I married my wife she enjoyed the trips as well as all the rest of our group. We then camped a lot with Melvin but my parents joined in as well. Each and every trip that we made was into the road less area of northern Minnesota or the road less area of Ontario Canada. All roads end at the edge of the wilderness.

Jay Johnson was an older fellow that I worked with so when he retired I told him that I would take him on a fishing trip to Canada instead of a retirement gift. This next poem is about his trip.

The Wilderness Trip

To Canada, Jay Johnson came,
With my son and I in a fishing game.
We fished the lakes so cold and deep
And come the night, in my bus we'd sleep.

It was the first trip there for Jay,
But he did well, I have to say.
He saw a life he'd not seen before,
As if he'd opened a new worlds door.

He saw the land thru a sports mans eye,
And vowed right there that he would try
To return next summer, with his wife along
So she could hear the wilderness song.

They did return but there was woe.
They made mistakes that really show.
They left their food in a tent there,
An invitation to a hungry bear.

It made a door where none had been,
Then made another one out again.
It ate the food, and ruined the tent,
Then to the woods again, it went.

When they returned and found this sight,
Jay knew they couldn't spend the night.
So they hurried home to tell their tale,
Of their adventure on the wilderness trail.

I enter this poem here, not to embarrass Jay, but as a demonstration to the reader, that if you have never been in the wilderness enough to know your way around, then stay with someone that can keep you out of trouble. You may feel that all of the adventures of life are safe now, but the wilderness will teach you a very cruel lesson. Jay and his wife were lucky, they weren't there when nature came calling.

This next poem was something I submitted to the "World of Poetry Magazine" and was awarded the title of "Silver Poet"

Living In The Woods

I live my life out in the woods,
Away from man made things.
To see the sights and hear the sounds
Of nature when it sings.

I hear the birds up in the trees
When dawn does first arrive.
They greet the sun with melodies
As the day does come alive.

The flowers in the morning mist
All sparkle from the dew.
Their colors range the spectrum,
From white, to pink or blue.

The bright green leaves upon the trees
Are beautiful to see.
As they rustle in the midday breeze,
And spread their shade for me.

The chorus of the frogs I hear
From the pond not far away,
Announce the coming of the night,
And the closing of the day.

I hear the loons as they swim about
In the middle of the night,
As they sing and dance across the waves
And tell me every things alright.

Northern Minnesota

The patter of the raindrops
On my tent at early dawn
Foretold of gloomy weather,
As mosquito's sang their song.

Just half awake I listened
As the woods awoke outside.
Heard the sounds of natures choir
When at singing the birds tried.

They sang not as a robin
That will greet the morning sun.
But instead with little twitters,
I could hear them one by one.

On this grey and rainy morning
The song they did compose,
Was not a song of gladness,
But their sadness did disclose.

Then of a sudden came a sound
That brought me wide awake.
T'was the haunting, chilling, laughter
Of a loon out on the lake.

It sang it's early morning song,
As the birds did on the shore,
To tell it's mate of springtime love.
As the rain began to pour.

The thunder and the lightning
Put on a brief display
As the rain fell down in torrents,
That washed the ground away.

Several hours later,
When the clouds at last did part.
The sunshine made its entrance,
That would gladden any heart.

The world began to sparkle
From each brightly shining drop,
That looked like tiny rainbows
With gold sunlight piled on top.

The birds now sang more sweetly
And with gladness in their voice.
As they called to one another
On this day that gave a choice.

I stood outside my canvas home,
On this pine covered isle.
I looked out o'er the jeweled lake,
On a day that made me smile.

The air was filled with freshness
From the flowers I could smell.
And the sweet and scented pine air
Fit in the picture well.

The lake lie still and quiet
As it mirrored the tree lined shore,
With nothing to disturb it
'Cept the loons, which numbered four.

They cruised across the water
To their favorite fishing spot.
And I felt as an intruder,
But my presence mattered not.

They dived and caught the minnows
That were swimming 'neath the waves.
While I stood and watched them spell bound,
To the scene I was a slave.

This is the scene I looked upon
That early summer morn
In Northern Minnesota
Where the wilderness is born.

Thru Minnesota's northern part of the state, lies the Superior National Forest. It stretches from just east of International Falls to the shores of the biggest lake on earth, Lake Superior. From the border it stretches south to Palo, Minnesota, some three and a half million acres. I'm fortunate enough to live next to this giant forest and I've played in it since I was a child. There are several thousand lakes within its boundaries and some of them are very large. One of the largest lies towards the eastern end and is one of the chain of lakes that make up the Minnesota, and Ontario, Canada border. This is the main route that the Voyageurs traveled when they were transporting supplies from the eastern cities of the U.S. and Canada to the settlements of north, and western Canada, and to a lesser degree, Washington. It was the heart of the fur trade, and without it progress would have taken much longer to open up that vast land.

The area along the Minnesota border, about twenty miles wide, is the Boundary Waters Canoe Area Wilderness. This is a totally road less area where no motors of any kind are allowed. On the Ontario side is the Quetico Park that also is road less and also has the same motor less restriction. Even air planes cannot fly over the area unless they are thousands of feet in the air.

When the voyageurs were working the line they would cross the Great Lakes until they reached Grand Portage, Minnesota. From there they would portage their ninety pound packs thru this chain of lakes all the way to Fort Athabasca in Saskatchewan. Most of them were small men because they all had to fit into the canoes that they hauled the freight in.
Because they were small does not mean they were weak as they normally carried two packs, and sometimes three, over the portages. These portages

were anything from a lift over a beaver dam, to several miles in length. Most of them however were more likely a half mile or less.

Once they arrived at the main chain of lakes that now form the International Border, one of the first lakes they came to is a lake that is called Saganaga, (pronounced sag na ga) As I said this lake is large but is not just a huge body of water. It has many points and bays, with depths more than one hundred feet, and huge rocks that stick up above the surface of the lake. It is not a lake to be taken lightly by the unaware. There is a small group of residences that live there year around but most people only visit for a short time in summer or winter to fish and hunt, and camp.

The original white people who lived there called the lake "The Lady"

Faces Of The Lady

As I awoke I smelled the smoke
Of my campfire burning low.
In my little camp on Saganaga
At the far end of the trail.
Where mankind meets the wilderness
And memories do prevail.

The sky was blue, the waters too,
As the sun like a sleepy eye,
Looked over the mirror of this watery world,
Where I'd go forth
To see again what this day would bring
On this Lady of the north.

I felt near blessed as there I dressed,
And added fuel to the fire.
While all around the birds did sound
With a morning symphony.
And the lapping of the tiny waves,
Made music just for me.

I stopped to smile for a little while,
As a scene then did unfold
Of a whitetail deer, with a pair of fawns,
As they came for their morning drink,
Then quickly fled to the woods around
In the space of an eye's blink.

Some fish I'd take from this jeweled lake
Before the day was thru,

But here on the shore in the mornings glow,
I hurried not at all.
Just sipped my tea, and ate my "jacks,"
And listened to natures call.

I left my camp with the dew still damp,
To paddle down the lake.
Past rocks and trees that are centuries old,
And majestic just to see.
When I heard a splash as a tail crashed,
From a beaver, that did see me.

Then up ahead, just turning red,
I see a wild strawberry,
And there in the rock, in a sheltered spot,
Are bushes with white flowers,
That soon will grow the blueberries,
Where the bears will feed for hours.

I paddle slow as on I go
Fishing here and there.
The walleye is the one I seek,
And I hope to make it mine.
Then I'll stop on shore to snack and snore,
While on my fish I dine.

Next, a turn I make across the lake
To a long and shallow bay,
Where grows the green pond Lilly,
That blooms in yellow and white,
That feeds the great horned moose
In the days fading twilight.

As the stars appear I again draw near
To my campsite on the isle.
Where I will sit by little fire
And listen to the songs
Of loons cruising on this lake
Where nature has no wrongs.

There was no fright on this moonless night
As the darkness gathered round.
I found my blankets and snuggled in,
Inside my dinky tent,
Where I said my prayers and closed my eyes,
And off to sleep I went.

And then a flash, and a booming crash,
As lightening walked about.
The rain that fell just passed on by,
Leaving puddles in its wake,
And I returned to peaceful sleep
Beside this northern lake.

In the mornings mist, the shore was kissed,
As the waves crashed against the rocks,
While the color of the slate grey sky,
Matched the waters down below,
And the rain that fell in silver sheets
Kept pace with the wind that blows.

There I lay at the break of day
Looking at this snarling demon.
Only a fool would paddle today,
Much better to stay ashore.
Why risk my neck and life and limb
When there's an island to explore.

With cup in hand, my day I planned,
Of the things that I would do.
Then I set out in the pouring rain
To see what I might find.
This lakes been home, to those who roam,
So I'll see what they left behind.

I wandered round the rocky ground
Past flowers and trees growing there
And gave my thanks to the one above
For putting me in this place.

The day just flew, until at last I knew,
I was back to my camping space.

This lands alive with the things that thrive
In this northern wilderness.
I'd like to stay but it's not allowed.
Out here I'm just a guest.
This Lady likes to live alone
Perhaps, this ways the best.

At crack of dawn I carry on
As I turn my canoe toward home.
I've seen two faces of the Lady,
Her moods are so unruly,
But day or night, wrong or right,
I love this Lady truly.

And right or wrong I sing this song,
As I leave the Lady now.
I'd love to think I'm needed there,
But I know it's just not so.
Next, I'll come back to another face,
When it's covered white with snow.

This next poem is about an old trappers shack I found in northern Ontario that not only was beautiful, but impressed me so much I took a picture and then had one of my sisters, who was a professional artist, paint it for me. This picture is hanging over my bed in my bedroom. The picture is well done, but still can not do true justice to the wonderful scene that it dominates. This shack is probably thirty miles from the nearest highway, and you would have to make many portages to arrive there.

The Place

An old deserted cabin stood lonely by the lake,
Near where the river emptied, at the backend of the bay.
With rocks and trees tucked all around,
An inviting place to stay.

The sun was low in the western sky
And the wind was but a breeze
That rippled the sparkling water
And made a sighing in the trees.

Around a point I made my way
Till I came upon the scene.
The nearest man was miles away,
This was wilderness serene.

I came alone to this fine place
Where I had never been before,
To just relax and catch some fish,
And maybe to explore.

I then lay down my paddle,
As the canoe slid on alone,
And I had a sudden feeling
That at last I had come home.

Somehow I felt so welcome,
As if the cabin there could speak,
While I sat and watched the sunsets glow
As it reached a rosy peak.

I pitched my tent upon the shore,
And made my little fire.
Then sat and dreamed of living there,
It was my one desire.

To live somewhere with nature
Has always been a dream.
And now I sat, alone, content,
and listened to the stream.

The lake was quiet, and like a mirror
Which reflected every tree.
While the river gurgled oe'r the rocks,
And sang a song for me.

The twilight came, and then the night,
As a loon called from afar,
While across the bay, a beaver swam,
His trail like a scar.

I slept then in my little tent,
Until the early morn,
When the birds awoke, and began to sing,
And a symphony was born.

The Robin, and the Blue Jay,
And the black capped Chickadee,
All sang their songs to greet the sun,
But I felt it was for me.

I spent the day there in this glen,
In the silence of the wood,
And dreamed my dream that some day
I could maybe stay for good.

It was a dream that couldn't be,
I had to leave quite soon,
But for that night it felt so real
There beneath the moon.

My time was gone I had to leave
To return to kith and kin,
But as I left I felt a void
Of emptiness within.

When I did leave, as days flew by
I vowed I would return,
And I'll keep this memory with me,
As a fire it will burn.

And when someday the time has come
To return to that grand place,
Though I may be old and bent with age,
There'll be a smile upon my face.

If after reading these lines you get the idea that I love this part of northern Minnesota, you are correct. The people of this area have fought, since they first got here, to protect it from the encroachment of the greedy ones who would turn it into a carnival and kill it within a very short time. This land is so fragile that we really do have to limit the number of people that are allowed to visit each year. It takes centuries for nature to remake one inch of soil. It takes less than one summer of campers to wear it away. The campsites are moved from spot to spot as needed to prevent this from happening. The number of days that each party is allowed to stay are also regulated.

While Minnesota is not the land of continuous ice and snow as some people think, it can be very changeable. In my lifetime I have seen it snow every month of the year. I have seen temperatures range from sixty below zero to one hundred plus. It is not a land to get careless in. Those of us that live here have learned to live with it, not to fight it. I want this land to remain forever for those who care for it. What will our great grandchildren have if we don't save it for them.

After I had married and had a wife and three children to care fore, I began to write, and think about, other things. Some times you just feel melancholy, then you begin to think of things you would not usually think about. Other times it is worry that causes you to have wandering thoughts. So it is here in these next two poems.

The Storm

The weather outside is a frozen blur
From the wind blown snow and cold.
The frost is thick on the window pane,
As the fear of a blizzard takes hold.

I sit and watch as the snow piles deep,
And the electric wires sag,
And I hear the ticking of the clock,
As the hours begin to drag.

The kids are away at school today,
My wife away at her job.
They should have come home hours ago,
As the snow comes down in gobs.

The radio says visibility is gone,
To travel is to risk your life.
The kids are on the bus I know,
But what about my wife?

The sky outside is really gray
As daylight comes to a close.
I hear the bus as the kids arrive,
They know to come home when it snows.

The kids all say the roads are bad,
The bus barely made it thru,
And I think of my wife out there,
And the worries start anew.

It's happened before when a storm has struck
She couldn't make it home,
She tried her best, but still she failed,
And she was stuck alone.

The last time was the worst of all,
When she followed the neighbors car,
Till he got stuck, and his car she struck,
And the cars were dented and scarred.

Or maybe it was the time before,
When she was forced off of the road,
Into snow so white in the fading light,
In a drift that the wind had blowed.

When her car then stalled,
Out the door she crawled,
To find herself alone,
In a frozen drift, and miles from a phone.

The snow around was piled in drifts,
The temperature was falling fast.
She knew her chance for help was gone,
As that last car went on past.

She sat alone in the freezing car,
As colder grew each moment,
Her frozen feet she tried to move,
But they were like cement.

At last some headlights did shine thru,
This screaming, deadly storm,
And a policeman told my freezing wife,
"Come in my car, where it is warm."

She made it back to safety
On that bleak and fearful night,
But when I finally got to her
She was a sorry sight.

Her cheeks were stained from frozen tears,
Her hair was all a mess,
She was so scared from her ordeal
That the police man I did bless.

I think of all these other storms,
As this one screams outside.
Perhaps I'd better go and see.
I think I'll take a ride.

I know which road she'll travel on,
I'll meet her with some luck,
She's got the car with the bald tires,
So I'll just take the truck.

I hurry into heavy clothes,
And take a quilt along,
The motor springs to sudden life,
And the radio sings a song.

I start out in the frozen dark,
The snow a blurring white,
But there's something in our drive way now,
And it's a welcome sight.

She's made it home, she's safe at last.
She made the trip alright.
I'll not worry about her again,
Until another stormy night.

THOUGHTS

Do you know what it' like to be all alone,
With your thoughts all running wild?
To sit and dream, of your thoughts and schemes
Of when you were just a child.

Of thoughts long gone, of things gone wrong,
Or things that happened right.
To spend your day in this pleasant way
Or to spend a hectic night.

If things you choose to think about
Were pleasant and made you gay,
The time just flies as in your eyes
You spend a happy day.

If your memories long with things gone wrong,
The time just seems to stop,
As dreams unfold, that take a hold,
And pull you from the top.

You can't fight back, there is no slack,
As they drag you thru the mire,
And once again your blood runs hot,
And your breath is like a fire.

You feel again, the wrong was done,
That you felt so unjust,
But put away that awful day,
To carry on you must.

Until at last, your dreams are past,
And control reigns again,
When happy memories are on their way,
And things go as you plan.

To tell some tale of a secret trail
That lives within your mind.
Of some small adventure,
Or small treasure that you did find.

To put these thoughts on paper,
So the memories can come clear,
Or record them on a piece of tape,
So all can see and hear,

Is like a giant movie,
Where the actors all play parts,
And to say the words you should have said,
That you felt within your heart.

To tell off those who should be told,
Or to admit when you were wrong,
It is so sweet with after thought,
To sing the proper song.

As time goes by, in your minds eye
You have this happy choice,
Not like our daily ups and downs
When we live with the words we voice.

As I write these lines of the happy times
That I spent as a child,
I also find I was unkind,
And sometimes acted wild.

I said some things, and did some deeds,
That should never have been done.
The hurt was unintentional,
I was only having fun.

For life has been a ball for me,
Or at least I thought it so,
As I've watched the greening of the grass,
Or the coming of the snow.

I've watched new birth in early spring,
And the finality of the fall.
And tried my best to just accept
And I've enjoyed it all.

Enjoyed it all? I must say yes,
As I reflect a bit,
Though at the time I didn't smile
At all I must admit.

I only smiled at certain spots,
Where I've stopped along the way,
I guess I couldn't smile then,
But it makes me smile today.

Some times are sad or even bad,
As we live them day to day,
But leave them lay for long enough,
And black will turn to grey.

Then soon or late the things we hate,
Will somehow turn out right,
And while we are not looking
They will slowly turn to white.

The times we feared and those we cheered,
Will mellow out with time,
And as we journey down the road,
They all turn out just fine.

They all are memories after while,
That we try hard to keep.
Some are kept right up on top,
And some are buried deep.

But up on top of memory lane,
Or buried deep below,
The thoughts are there to come again,
Like winter with it's snow.

The happy thoughts we all enjoy,
They are as summer breezes,
The darker thoughts from down below,
Are more like winters freezes.

But I dwell not on thoughts unkind
When thinking of my youth.
So when I write of happy times,
I only speak the truth.

To tell of all the things I did
As I journeyed on my way,
And came at last to where I am,
As I write these lines today.

One day as I was in a reflective mood I began to think of other things. I've always wondered if the American Indians possibly knew more than white people gave them credit for. They believed that virtually everything had a life even if it was a rock. I expanded on this idea, and wondered if things that man builds don't also take on a life of their own. With this in mind I wrote this.

The Old House

One day while traveling a forgotten trail
The daylight grew short, as rain did prevail.
I had traveled since the early light,
Now I sought a place to spend the night.

Around the bend and there alone,
Stood an empty house made out of stone.
The front gate was broken, and hung awry
And the weeds in the yard reached for the sky.

The windows were broken, and the door stood ajar,
All this I could see from a distance far.
As I drew nearer, the neglect the more plain,
But it drew like a magnet, that I cannot explain.

I stood at the gate in the fading twilight,
Then I hurried inside, where I'd spend the night.
As I walked thru the door a feeling arose
That I'd be safe here, when the stormy wind blows.

It was knee deep in litter, with cob webs and dust,
The stove in the corner was covered with rust.
The lamp on the table was a most welcome sight,
So I cleaned it and lit it, to push back the night.

I wandered the house thru, to the bedrooms out back,
Till I felt at home in this tumbled down shack.
Then I lit a fire in the stove I did see,
And fried up some bacon, and boiled my tea.

As I sat by the fire, and the warmth did creep in,
I felt a great comfort, that came from within,
The house was my home, at least for the night,
So I spread my blankets, and blew out the light.

When all of a sudden, quite clear like a bell,
The house said to me, "I've a story to tell."
I looked all around for the voice in the gloom
But I was alone, there in that room.

I jumped to my feet, and I nearly ran,
But then I sat down, and the story began
"You've come unto me like a child to its mother,
So I'll tell you my story, that is like no other.

The family that built me and filled me with love,
Have all now passed on, to their home up above.
Then I had new owners that filled me with life,
Some times with love, sometimes trouble and strife.

I've had brand new babies that were born in my room,
And twice evil folks have in here met their doom.
I've seen new romance take a root hold and grow,
Then wither and die, like the springs melting snow.

I've seen little children grow up to be men,
And then I've been filled with children again.
I've seen them grow old and just fade away,
And I'd be alone, until someone else came to stay.

Now I've been empty for many a year
With no one to care if I just disappear.
My windows are broken, and my door doesn't close,
And the snow does come in when the winter wind blows.

I'd be oh so happy to hold a family once more,
If they'd fix up my windows, and brace up my floor,
Paint up my woodwork and clean out the dirt,
I'd sure do my best to keep them from hurt.

But I guess I'm too old to be use full again,
Except, when a traveler has a night time to spend.
I thank you for staying, you've treated me well
And thank you for listening to the story I tell"

I sat there amazed, my head filled with wonder,
While the darkness around me shook with the thunder,
A summer time storm was now passing by,
But here in this house I remained safe and dry.

I seemed wide awake, but must not have been,
For of a sudden I knew it was daylight again,
The night had passed by, and the hours had flown,
But if I slept or not was a fact still unknown.

My head must have nodded, my eyes must have shut,
I must have fallen asleep there in that hut,
I must have been sleeping, how else to explain,
A house that tells stories, at night in the rain.

I looked out the window at the early dawn,
And said to my self, it's time I move on.
I gathered my gear, and walked out neath the sky,
When a voice from with in, whispered "Goodbye"

The Family

At the edge of our little town,
A house there does stand
With no houses around,
That is the way it was planned.

This house all alone
Stands high on a hill,
With a creek down below
Running quiet and still.

There are trees in the yard,
But no birds do there sing,
They're all frightened away
By the laughter that rings.

The yard has no care,
It's all thistles and weeds,
But it's just fine with us
As it fulfills our needs.

No folks will you find
From our little town,
Because they all wish
It were all torn down.

This house is so old,
Built in 1904,
With windows and shutters
And a big oaken door.

This is the home
Of Mabel and me,
With all of our children
Which number three.

All of their offspring
Live here as well
So sometimes at night
You may hear them yell.

Some folks call them crazy,
As well they may be,
But we love them the same,
Mabel and me.

The people from town
Just don't come around,
They're afraid of the noise,
And unusual sounds.

They stay far away,
And warn their children as well,
To never come near
What they all call "Hell".

What they all call "Hell"
Is our family home,
And far from this place
We never will roam.

We're happy you see
Here in this house,
Where our only pet
Is an over sized mouse.

Of course, there are bats
That hang in the hall,
But they're all gone at night,
So don't bother at all.

We sleep all the day
As we can't stand the sun,
So it's always at night
That we have our fun.

We all screech and howl
As we bay at the moon,
Because as you know,
Daylights coming too soon.

By now you can see
That we don't live as most
And that's why no one wants us
As an over night host

I've tried to explain,
But I don't get my choice,
Because they all run away
When they hear my voice.

We mean you no harm,
That is my boast,
It's just the way that we are,
This family of ghosts.

There's Jimmy you see,
Who is just three feet tall,
And his brother Tommy
Who is the tallest of all.

Mary's the girl
With only one arm.
She was caught by a bear,
That meant her great harm.

Sally's the girl
With the prettiest eyes,
But her mind is destroyed,
So she often time cries.

Bobby's the one
Who often times screams
When strangers appear,
Though they're seldom seen.

Alfred, my son
Has the most fun of all.
If someone comes near
He makes things fall.

Tillie, my oldest,
Takes care of me
Because I am blind,
So I cannot see.

Suzy, my youngest,
Likes to play in the park,
To scare normal folks
Out there in the dark.

And then there is Mabel,
The mother of all,
Who makes windows rattle
When to us she does call.

So this is our family
That does live in this house,
But if you come to visit,
You'll see the over sized mouse.

CHAPTER EIGHT

When I was but a boy we lived on a farm just west of Long Lake, Minnesota. Our house stood about one hundred yards from the Great Northern Railroad tracks. Although this was after the Great Depression was officially over, there still were a lot of people out of work, and guys out on the bum were common. These men were mostly hobo's and were offended if you called them a "Bum". A hobo was a man that was honest and was actively looking for work to support his family. A Bum was an unscrupulous individual who thought the world owed him a living.

These hobo's were following the railroads in the hope of being able to "hop" a freight train to transport them to where ever they thought they wanted to go. Since our house was so close to the tracks, it was a convenient place to ask for food in return for work. Though we never had much to eat ourselves, my mother always gave them what we had. I don't remember any of them ever complaining about what she gave them to eat. They always did more than enough work around the place to more than pay for what they ate. I remember one time Mother was canning when one fellow came, and Mother told him that she had to finish what she was doing first. He asked if he could help. He helped her with the project that she was on, then suggested that they move on to more canning. She happily got most of her canning done that day. Finally it was time for supper, so she told him that he could eat with us. He refused, saying that it wouldn't be right for him to eat with "decent folks". After a lot of discussion he finally agreed. While we were eating he told us that he was from Ohio and hadn't been home for over a year. "He just sent what money he made to his wife." He said that he always had helped his wife and so he really appreciated my mother letting him help.

When these men would stop in, they would always tell us what life was like on the road. I suppose that was where a part of my wanderlust came from. Recalling those days got me to thinking about this next poem.

Momma's Boy

In the freight yards of Chicago
Some men had gathered round
A feeble fire of sticks and leaves
They'd built there on the ground.

December rain was falling
On this dank and dreary day,
But the men stood quiet and listened,
To what the old man had to say.

He said "I've been out bummin
Now for fifty years and more.
But it hardly seems a lifetime,
Since I left my Momma's door."

The day I left was painful,
Like the other days gone by,
Cause my Father and my Brother
Always made me cry.

They beat me and abused me
And called me "Momma's Boy"
Because I always did my best for her
By using every ploy.

I'd run her little errands,
Or of an evening, I'd hold her hand
Till Daddy soon did call me
"Momma's Little Man".

Brother too was jealous
If I brought our Mother joy,
And he would kick and beat me
While he called me "Momma's Boy".

In dark of night they'd come to me,
And use me as a whore,
Until the day that I left home,
I couldn't stand it any more.

Then I set out to ride the rails
And forget my wicked past,
But joy has been so fleeting
It just never seemed to last

I looked for peace within my self
And tried to find life's joy
But in my mind I'd hear the words
You're just a "Momma's Boy".

Then one day a year ago
I met a childhood friend,
Who opened up my troubled mind,
Many hours we did spend.

He made me see I'd done no wrong,
The fault had not been mine,
My father and my brother
Were the ones that made the crime.

They alone must answer
For the awful things they've done,
Alone in front of Gods great throne
There'll be no place to run.

So I've been gone these many years,
And have lived my life alone,
But tonight I made my mind up,
Tomorrow, I'll go home.

To see my dear old "Momma",
And to hold her close and say,
"Though I've been gone these many years,
I've missed you every day".

I want to see her smile,
And I'm not acting coy,
For it really will not matter
Who calls me "Momma's Boy"

The other men just stood there
As the old man walked away.
They knew they couldn't let him,
Go home on that next day.

His Mothers' gone to her reward
Many years ago.
His father and his brother too,
Are lying neath the snow.

So all that's left for this old man
To maybe bring him joy,
Are friends in an old freight yard,
Who won't call him "Momma's Boy."

This next one just shows how sometimes we set out to do the proper thing after a wrong has been committed, and how we sometimes never get around to doing what we should at the time.

The Old Man

I met a man so old and grey
As I was passing on my way.
So I stopped to talk and rest a while,
With this old man whose eyes did smile.

We sat and talked of many things,
In the trees above the birds did sing,
He told of life when he was young.
The words just rolled from off his tongue.

He told me oh, so many tales
Of things he'd done, along life's trails.
It seemed he had so much to say,
This smiling man with beard of grey.

He spoke about the days of old,
And of a maiden with hair of gold,
Of how they met, and later wed.
I longed to hear each word he said.

He told me of the work he'd done.
Life for him had all been fun.
That he had lived a merry life,
With two fine sons, and a pretty wife.

Then he stopped his talk, and gazed a space,
As a look of sadness crossed his face.
There is one tale I've never told,
He said to me as his eyes turned cold.

He told me then another tale
That happened to him along life's trail.
He said he had another son,
Back in the days when he was young.

Though he was wed, and wore a ring.
With another girl he'd had a fling.
She bore a son with no last name
And ever since she'd lived in shame.

He'd probably be as old as you,
With your brown hair and eyes of blue.
I cannot guess as to his size,
I've never seen him, with my own eyes.

I've never met this other son,
For far away the girl did run.
I've always hoped to meet the lad
Were the final words the old man said'

We sat in silence till I did say,
I'd best be getting on my way.
I've rested here and heard your tale,
But Its time for me to hit the trail.

The old man nodded, but in his eye,
A look of sadness I did spy.
Be on your way to journeys end
But come again when you've time to spend.

I thought maybe you were my son,
When you listened to the tale I've spun.
I hoped you'd tell me of your mother,
And did she ever find another?

I said, I'm sorry, it's not mine to say,
What happened to her after that day,
See, mothers gone long years ago
And I knew not, where I should go.

I gave my word in a promise true,
That I'd return when I passed thru.
I've not returned to that resting place,
To see the man with the bearded face.

He died next day, so I've been told,
This grey old man so bent and old.
I know not why he told to me,
His tale of life and tragedy.

So now I live with this inside
This tale that so long did hide.
I didn't tell him, I didn't bother
To tell the man, he was my Father.

Because this country was settled nearly one hundred years before I arrived, and not all homesteads were located in places where people could actually make a living, there are still old homesteads in very odd places. One day when I was wandering in the woods, miles from any road I ran across one of the old farmsteads. As I wandered around the old yard, I found a small area that obviously had been fenced. It was approximately four feet by six feet and there were the remains of an old fence. I thought at first the it was possibly some ones flower bed that they were protecting from the deer and rabbits.

After farther investigation I realized that it was a private grave yard. I scratched around in the weeds and leaves until I found an old board that someone had carved. After cleaning it a little I made out two names. I found a solid stick that would work, then removing one of my boot laces I tied the stick and board together and planted it there on the graves.

This is the story as I remember it now.

Billy Joe And Ruth

One day as I was walking,
Many years ago.
I came upon a mystery
(Or at least I thought it so.)

I'd wandered far through out the day,
Over hill and dale.
Through forest green, and meadows fair,
Down a long and dusty trail.

In a clearing in the forest,
Standing all alone,
An old forgotten homestead,
That once had been a home.

Sometime, someone had lived there,
And had built it all by hand,
When they had made their living,
From the poor and swampy land.

Though grown up with weeds and brush
The signs were there to read.
There once had been a barn and well,
For the livestock they would need.

Off to the side I found the base
Of what once had been a shed.
Where they had raised some chickens,
To go with their daily bread.

A garden spot I found there next,
Though it was over grown,
With weeds and grass and other things
That the wind had surely blown.

Then near the top of a little hill,
In a little fenced in pen,
I read the tale of their lives there,
And how things there had been.

Two little graves lie side by side,
Of a little girl and boy.
That spoke to me of sadness,
Instead of heart felt joy.

The marker that I found there
Said they were six and five,
And told about the years and days,
When they had been alive.

But told me naught about the cause,
That put them in the ground.
And not a clue it offered me
Where their parents could be found.

I wandered round that clearing twice,
But could not find a trace,
To tell me of the tragedy
That must have taken place.

Was it disease or accident
That took their lives away,
And who was it that put them there,
On this hillside where they lay

These questions nearly drove me mad
As I tried to find the truth.
To tell me of the tragic end
Of "Billy Joe and Ruth".

Now the years have flown away
And I still don't know the tale,
Of what happened in that little field
At the end of that long trail.

Thinking back on all the jobs I've held throughout my life I really have to smile. Some have been good jobs and some have been a pain in the neck. I've been a farmer, a forest fire fighter, an electrician all over this country and Canada. I've driven trucks and busses all over the U.S. and Canada and for a while I drove tour busses all over the U. S., Mexico, and Canada. It was a fun job, but one that demanded a lot of actual work, taking care of the passengers, and the bus. I also had to take care of my trucks when I drove them but I usually enjoyed the work more. It was during my truck driving days that I came up with this next poem. This is strictly a figment of my imagination but it could have happened.

The Woman Who Wasn't There

One night while driving a lonesome road,
In a tired old truck with a heavy load,
Thru the wind and rain I saw a sight
That no one should see on a cold dark night.

A car in the ditch in front of me
With a person inside that I could see.
I had to stop to lend a hand
Cause no one moved in this lonesome land.

When out of the door, a woman came
With snow white hair, and a walk that was lame.
I thought she would fall as she climbed up the bank,
Then I saw she was hurt, and my heart sank.

The nearest town was miles away,
And I had traveled far that day.
I needed to rest, my prayer was for sleep,
But this old woman was in trouble deep.

She's hurt and alone I thought with a sigh,
And I can't leave her here, so I'll have to try
To take her along to the town up ahead,
If she makes it that far, before she is dead.

She climbed into the cab without saying a word,
With no indication that my questions she heard.
I asked for her name without a reply.
Then I asked "can you talk" but she wouldn't try.

I wondered aloud if deafness was there,
But she gave me a cold, icy stare.
That look alone made me understand
That she wanted no more of this barren land.

So I pulled it in gear and drove off in the night
To get her some help, or try as I might.
I drove on for hours, but no people I found
While the old woman sat without making a sound.

Then gravel did fly up under my truck,
And I knew right away, I'd run out of luck.
"I'm falling asleep" I cried with alarm,
So I have to stop before I cause you more harm.

Then out of the night some people appeared,
And helped down the woman, but no voices I heard.
They took her to a house that stood there,
And I saw her no more with her snow colored hair.

I crawled into the back and quickly did snore.
Thoughts of the woman didn't bother me more,
Until I awoke to the shining sunlight
To a scene around me, that gave me a fright.

There in the ditch ahead was the car,
From which I had driven so very far,
And there in the car was the snowy white head
Of a tired old woman who was lying there dead.

Now there was no house for miles around,
And no tracks from people were there on the ground.
No way to tell we'd traveled all night.
No answer I found, try as I might.

No answer either as I walked to the car,
To find it now empty, with the front door ajar.
So I ran to my truck, and got out of there
When there on the seat, I found a long white hair.

In days gone by the people that lived north of the forty eighth parallel have relied on the use of dogs to transport their gear and themselves from place to place. The Laplanders and parts of Russia and Scandinavia also used reindeer, but it was predominately dogs. Since the invention of the snowmobile there is less and less use of the dogs. However many of these people have kept their dogs for recreational purposes. These dogs are used for racing on a known course. The largest of these races are run in Canada, and Alaska. There are also races in the northern U. S. and some of them require just as much endurance, and as much danger as the races that are run farther north. One such race is run near the north shore of Lake Superior. It is entirely within the state of Minnesota and many of the "mushers" have commented to the press, that this is a tougher course than the fabled Iditarod in Alaska. It is not nearly as long but it is much more hilly, and hard on the dogs and the mushers. When the race was first began back in the 1970's the big name mushers would compete in this race. After three years of trying they all quit coming because it was to hard for dogs that were expected to move on to other races during the racing season.

This race is called "The Beargrease". It begins and ends in Duluth, Minnesota. It originally had a course of five hundred miles but in recent years it has been shortened to four hundred. Again because the Terrain is too rough on the dogs and mushers. This course is run on what is called the Canadian Shield, which is an outcropping of the granite that composes a great deal of central Canada. The ground level of this area is very broken. It is covered with trees, wherever they chose to grow, with numerous creeks and rivers running into Lake Superior. These water courses are generally from ten to fifty feet below the general lay of the land. Therefore the dogs are either running uphill or downhill for the entire course. The mushers are pretty well in the position of running the entire course as well because there are not many miles where the musher can ride the sled. This is definitely not a course for sissies.

The race takes it's name from an Indian named John Beargrease that used to deliver mail from Duluth, to Grand Marais, Minnesota, long before there ever was a road in that country. In fact the first road thru this part of Minnesota wasn't completed until 1925.

A friend decided he wanted to run dogs, and he trained for over a year before he decided to attempt the race. He is the one I wrote this poem about.

The Beargrease

Into the night he rode, alone,
On the runners of his sled,
Down the trail of frozen snow,
While the stars danced overhead.

Five more teams were up ahead,
And eleven more behind,
As he mushed the "Beargrease Trail,"
Four hundred miles to unwind.

The night was cold, and the miles long,
As his breath froze to his beard,
And the creak and groan of the sliding sled
Were the sounds the musher heard.

Of course there was the panting too
From sixteen sets of lungs,
Of fifteen dogs, and a running man,
As the night around them hung.

He'd ride the sled when ere he could,
As downhill they would speed,
But run and push his share and more,
Whenever came the need.

He'd left Duluth at evening time,
And left the lights aglow,
And raced along with just the moon
Reflecting on the snow.

There was a lamp upon his head,
But he seldom turned it on,
To check his dogs, or find a turn
On this trail that "Beargrease" spawned.

They ran that way, thru night and day,
With rest stops now and then,
Until at last at Grand Marias,
An eight hour sleep they'd spend.

Then turn them running dogs around
And race against the clock,
Two hundred miles of ice and snow,
All frozen like a rock.

The temperatures in the frozen zone
As they ran with all their might,
Prevented them from sweating
As they ran all day and night.

He watched the traces carefully
To see if there was slack.
He needed every ounce of pull,
To make the trip on back.

If a dog was ill, or had its fill
Of pulling night and day,
He'd leave it at a check point,
Then continue on his way.

By now his team was tired out
And pulling just with heart
As he came at last back to Duluth
Where the race, had had its start.

And as they sprinted across the line
He knew they'd done their best
And he, along with his tired dogs,
Had passed the "Beargrease" test.

CHAPTER NINE

I think everyone has a master that we are a slave too. Most people deny such a thing as it normally is lying somewhere where it is not exposed. The common ones that are readily recognized are the easy ones such as smoking, drinking, gambling and so on, the common ones that are not readily recognizable are such things as perfectionism, my son has this master, sloppiness, and so on. My master is, and always has been, fishing. I can't begin to tell how many times I've had important tasks to perform when the sudden urge to go fishing has struck, and off I would go to some lake or river. The only thing that would come close to being a match is my willingness to eat everything in sight. Even when I'm fishing I have to have something along to nibble on.

As much as I love sunfish, and sunfishing, in my latter years, I've pursued the walleye all over the northern states and Canada. They are great fish to catch and eat when they are taken out of the cold clear lakes of this region. I have never been the best or smartest walleye fisherman. Almost without fail, if my wife and I go fishing together, she will catch many more fish than I do. I tell her that it is because when I'm running the boat I am the guide, and she's the client. Every good guide will tell you that their job is to put their client on a good fishing site and then to help the client catch fish. Therefore I'm doing my job and putting her in the perfect spot. She doesn't believe me either.

On numerous occasions I've been in the same boat with two or three others, and have had them all out fish me even though we were using identical tackle and using bait from the same pail. That's just the way it is.

I realize that some days are good and others are perfect, but why are they good or perfect for the other people in the boat, and not me. I've had my days when I've caught more fish than what I could possibly take home and eat, but they have always been on days when I'm alone. My Dad always told me it was because I had eaten the wrong thing for breakfast. For lack of any other excuse, it is the one I normally use.

The Fish Are Biting

One winters day I decided to go
To fish thru the ice, on a lake I do know.
I took along Dad, as I would often do
To join in the fun, and catch some fish too.

Standing alone on a frozen lake
Is not the first choice that many men make.
It's not too much fun when the winter wind blows,
And Jack Frost is nipping your ears and your nose.

Two men together will talk and will walk
From one to the other, to see what has been caught.
Some good natured chatter will fly in the air,
And they will stay warm when the weather is fair.

So we traveled then in my old car,
To Salo lake that was not very far.
Then onto the ice we take did take a stroll
Where we kicked back the snow, and drilled a nice hole.

Then another hole I drilled, just for me,
And then I drilled several more, cause I like to roam free.
Dad started to fish, as I did as well,
As the sun came up and cast a magic spell.

Then my bobber went down as I pulled the line tight
And as I set the hook, the fish started to fight.
It pulled and it tugged, and made a long run
As I smiled with glee, this fishing is fun.

The fish finally tired and I pulled it on ice.
This five pound Northern was healthy and nice.
I thought of how this fish would fit in the pan.
As my wife cooked it for supper, that was my plan.

As I looked at my fish with my hook in its maw
I thought of the teeth in that powerful jaw.
Its white teeth were gleaming as it looked up at me,
Still ready to fight, this I could see.

As I reached for my hook the fish snapped his jaw tight
With my thumb inside, not a pretty sight.
I howled with pain as the fish thrashed about,
Then Dad did arrive and knocked the fish out.

As I withdrew my thumb, with the blood running free,
I was not as injured as I thought I would be.
Then Dad took a look and I heard him say
"I guess you just proved, the fish are biting today."

Some times I get funny ideas in my head and I sit down and write things that are not only pure fantasy, but are near impossible to believe. I think poems like that are mostly signs of my unstable mind but I wouldn't want it any other way. This is the way that I escape the humdrum, every day world. If a person can't imagine things like this, then I think they are missing out on life.

Fried Fish

I'd been on the road for many a day,
Across desert, valley, and plain,
When there in the road a little town
Was sleeping in the rain.

There on the left was the funeral home,
There on the right was a bar,
But I was looking for something to eat
Because I had traveled so far.

No folks did I see in this little town
As I drove from end to end.
Finally a sign said food and drinks
So some money, I thought I would spend.

A parking spot was right in front
So I parked, and walked on inside
The food I could smell, smelled mighty good
And it was something fried.

I picked up a menu and sat at a table
To see their bill of fare.
Suddenly a voice I heard,
From an old woman standing there.

She said all I've got is fish for tonight
It's late and about time to close.
I said that will work, if fresh it may be,
So it does not offend the nose.

So I gave her my order,
She nodded, then just disappeared.
And suddenly back again with a fish,
That she had just recently speared

She asked if this was fresh enough
With a voice that was all cracked with age.
I said that indeed, it would suit me quite well.
She said "I'll just sprinkle on some sage.

The fish that she brought was a golden brown,
So I just couldn't wait.
The lady that brought it just smiled,
As I sat there and cleaned up my plate.

Then suddenly I seemed to just nod off,
I fell asleep there in my chair.
I must have gotten up and left,
But if I did, I know not where.

When I awoke I found myself
Back on the desert plain.
So I started my car and drove down the road
Till I came to a town once again.

There on the left was a funeral home,
There on the right was a bar.
And there was a man walking down the street
Towards the café which was not far.

The building was shuttered, and falling down,
The sign and the walkway as well.
I asked the young man of another café,
And he said "I've a story to tell.

There is no café in this little town,
There's not been for thirty long years.
When I told him about last night,
The man broke down into tears.

That was my grandma that you speak about,
I'll bet that she served you fish.
After she asked if it was fresh enough
As you ate it there, from your dish.

I said that indeed, that was the meal,
That she served there to me.
He said "and I'll bet she took your wallet as well"
If you will just take time to see.

I looked, and sure enough it's gone,
Now I'm as dry as a bone.
He said the least I can do,
Is apologize, then I'll drive you on home.

I said I can't go, I'm out of fuel.
He said don't worry, it's happened before.
If you'll just show me which way to go
I'll bring you right to your door.

We hooked my car on behind his
And traveled all thru the day.
I finally smiled and said,
"right there is my drive way."

As he left I was waving goodbye
When I got a sudden fright.
There as he drove down the road
From me, he disappeared from sight.

When I walked in my house I found,
I broke right down and cried.
There on my chair lay my wallet
With everything still inside

I just can't explain why I feel this way
But I have a sudden rage
To have some fresh fish, fried golden brown
Sprinkled with a little sage.

The Little Girl

While camping near the shore,
Of a northern wilderness lake,
I thought I'd go exploring
And a fish I'd try to take.

My canoe I loaded with all my gear,
I'd return I knew not when.
Maybe I'd go to the end of the lake,
And then return once again.

Maybe I'd find a nice portage,
And travel on to see
If other lakes or rivers
Were out there calling me.

The lake was calm as I paddled on
To bays I'd never known.
Where I saw the writings on the rocks,
Of men whose time has flown.

Twenty miles I paddled that day.
Not one fish had I caught.
But I had food a plenty,
So it really mattered not.

I camped that night on a little isle,
And built my little fire.
To lay on my bed, and just relax,
That was my one desire.

As I lay awake in my little tent
I thought I could hear a voice,
To go and find where it was at,
I really had no choice.

I woke to find the morning sun
Sparkling on the dew.
And telling me to hurry on,
There are many things to do.

I drank my tea, and washed my face
Then paddled on my way.
This lake just had so much to see
As I journeyed on that day.

Something was calling. I knew not where,
And I knew not what it said,
As I traveled on between rocks and isles
Down this lake where the voice has led.

Finally I came to an old portage,
That was grown over with weeds.
The trees and brush grew thick in spots
But the portage served my needs.

Then onto the water once again,
Of a sparkling little pond.
This was not the end of this great portage
I would travel on beyond.

At last I came to a lake so blue,
It's water crystal clear,
It was on this lake somehow I knew
I'd find the voice, that I could hear.

I paddled on around a point
Of this lake so still and deep,
On past islands large and small
Till I heard a small voice weep.

There on the shore I found a scene
Of a terrible tragedy.
A small plane crashed in the rocks and trees,
And a small voice calling me.

A small young girl, only eight years old,
Was the only one alive.
Her foot was trapped in the wreckage there,
But she had struggled to survive.

I used a stick as a lever then
To lift the tangled mess.
She pulled her foot out then,
It was worse than you would guess.

Her Mother and her Dad were gone,
Onto their final end.
She alone had struggled on,
For the three days she did spend.

I took her away in my canoe,
Away from that gruesome sight.
She cried, and called for her mom and dad
As I sat and held her tight.

I tried to explain thru her hurt and pain,
That her Mother and Dad were gone.
That her foot would heal, and she would feel,
That someday she could move on.

I cleaned her up and put her to bed,
There in my little tent.
As I sat by my little fire,
A sleepless night I spent.

We started out next day for home,
To find her kith and kin,
They never even gave their thanks,
But I'd do it all again.

This little girl with the golden hair,
And her sparkling eyes of blue
Shouted to me as they took her away.
Some day I'll be back, and I'll marry you.

Some things just don't turn out as you expect as this next poem shows.
Sometimes the surprises number more than just one.

The Girl Came Back

At last the girl is coming back.
I've waited ten long years.
I didn't want to lose her then,
There were too many tears.

I'd pulled her out of a bad plane crash,
In a wilderness serene.
Where she'd been trapped for three long days
In conditions most obscene.

Then I carried her for three more days,
When all she did was cry.
To bring her back to be repaired
I did my best to try.

But bring her back I did with glee,
Until that fateful day,
When kith and kin they did arrive,
And took the girl away.

She's coming back this very day,
My heart is all aglow,
She's coming back to marry me,
Her letters tell me so.

Now she is coming from the bus,
I'd know her anywhere,
There are the sparkling eyes of blue,
And there's her golden hair.

She hasn't seen me yet I'm sure,
She's looking all about.
Now she sees me standing here,
And she calls me with a shout.

Hey, old man, have you seen Tom,
He's supposed to meet me here?
I bit my tongue, and held my voice,
O'er the words that I did hear.

My name is Tom, I finally said,
My voice was filled with pain.
I'm the one you left ten years ago,
Perhaps I should explain.

You were so very young back then,
On that tragic fateful day.
You didn't notice that I was old,
Already turning gray.

I'm sorry I'm old and a surprise,
I don't mean to make you cry.
But you're standing there with a smiling face,
And you'll probably say "good bye."

She said, "old man," you're wrong again,
I'm not who you thought I'd be.
Barbara's at home under doctors care,
But I'm standing here to see.

I said, old girl we've both been wrong,
But can we settle this together?
Let's just sit down to a glass of beer
And talk about the weather.

You talk about the weather, old man,
But I'll just talk about us.
I wrote the letters that you loved
So let's not make a fuss.

I came here to wear a dress,
And stand right by your side,
So if you still want me, old man,
I'll be your blushing bride.

You'll be my bride, why I just don't know,
I'd have to know you better.
You're cute and witty, that much I know,
But can you write a letter?

Write a letter to you? Sweet man,
Why I'm right before your eyes.
So hold me and kiss me, and tell me you care,
And you'll see where my heart lies.

I'm not the girl you saved that day,
And I guess I'll never be.
But I fell in love with your letters, old man,
And you fell in love with me.

I'm not in love with you dear girl,
I didn't write at all,
The letters were written by my youngest son,
And he's waiting for your call.

But let's go meet the handsome lad,
Who's waiting with open arms,
I'm sure you'll be happy with what you see,
As will he, with all of your charms.

They met and fell in love that day,
And there'll be a wedding soon.
My wife and I are happy as kids
As we walk beneath the moon.

Sometimes I just feel I should write some things just to make you laugh. This is the case with the next poem. I was trying to decide what to write next when my wife walked in with a cup of tea. As we were talking I noticed her feet were bare as it was near bedtime. I thought to my self that I would know her feet anywhere, and from any other feet. Most peoples' feet are distinctive in some way or another. Thinking that, inspired me to write this poem.

Feet

Just a little northeast of nowhere
Is the town where I abide.
With my lovely wife, and children,
Standing by my side.

This little town where we do live,
Is known not at all.
We don't encourage tourists
Until the snow begins to fall.

You see, the women here go naked
While the men wear what they please,
And the only law there is here is,
"No looking above the knees."

It's peoples feet that we do see,
Be they large, or small, or painted.
Some are ugly, some are cute,
And some are downright tainted.

We know each other by our feet,
It's a wondrous way to go.
Until the winter comes around,
When they're hidden neath the snow.

In winter time the women
Wear some frilly things,
And when they go down to Duluth,
They even wear their rings.

There were some lovely feet one day,
That walked right up to me,
The prettiest feet I'd ever seen,
And looking is still free.

I asked them what their name was,
They told me Josie Sweet.
Then I noticed there were rings
Upon these dainty feet.

I fell in love right then and there.
These beauties made me weep.
I said I've got to know this girl,
So, I'll just take a peep.

There stood a man about eight feet tall,
With a little woman's voice.
I guess I stopped and stared at him,
But I really had no choice.

He was ugly clear to the bone
His hair was all awry.
His beard was full of maggots.
This nearly made me cry.

He said, I've just moved to your little town.
So, if you will be my friend,
We can live together.
Happy hours we will spend.

I said, I'm sorry, I'm taken,
As my wife is quick to say.
So if we ever meet again,
I'll just turn away.

I shouldn't look above the knees,
That's not my normal plan,
But if I ever look again,
I hope it's not another man.

The Bottle On The Bar

As I walked into the bar that night,
I found there'd been a terrible fight.
Blood and hair lay all around,
And broken bottles did abound.

Two groups of men were in the bar,
One group was near, the other far,
With blackened eyes and whisky breath,
Some looked like they were near to death.

I asked a man what caused this fight,
That must have lasted half the night.
He looked at me with bloodied nose,
And a beaten body from head to toes.

He said, you see that bottle on the bar?
That's clear as any canning jar,
There's liquor there as you can see,
Now see if you agree with me.

How full is bottle standing there?
Just let your answer fill the air.
From out the dark there came a voice,
Said, Stranger, please don't make a choice.

This bloody fight's come to an end
So please don't start it up again.
To answer now is trouble plenty,
One says half full, one says half empty.

Here is another example of how my mind seems to wander sometimes. I was sitting here resting my eyes for a minute when this popped into my head.

Loves Frustration

I know a man whose name is Mike.
He has a daughter I really like.
I'd like to make her all my own,
And give to her, a happy home.

I said I'd love her all my life
If she will marry and be my wife,
I'll give to her everything's she's seen
Because this girl will be my Queen.

This girl has beauty beyond compare
With big green eyes and auburn hair.
She is tall, and long of limb,
And her voice is soft, like a fine church hymn.

She says she loves me, I believe it's true.
I reply, that I love her too.
She'll often sit upon my knee,
And we will share a kiss or three.

I love this girl with all my heart,
But her mother tries to keep us apart.
You see how I'm in a terrible fix
Cause this girl is four, and I'm just six.

My Love

As I awake in the morning mist
And see the Rose that has been kissed
By the evening dew, from the night before,
I think of love with you once more.

I think of love every now and then
As I think of you, and the time we spend.
It is so dear and precious to me
That I want you to know that I still love thee.

Each day I spend apart from you
Makes me lonely and oh so blue.
We really shouldn't be apart,
It ruins my day and breaks my heart.

To be together day by day,
With all the cares along the way,
Is like a tonic that I need
As on your love is where I feed.

We should always be together
And should we be apart? NO NEVER.
Your love is like the breath of spring,
It makes me happy, it makes me sing.

It makes me smile, and laugh out loud,
And being with you makes me proud.
When I'm with you is my greatest time
To know I'm yours, and you are mine.

My happiness depends on you
As I write these lines which are so true.
Please say you'll come and stay with me
Where I'll love you, and we'll be free.

Our happiness is on its way
When we have that wonderful day,
When we join hands and walk so proud
As if we're walking on a cloud.

I'll kiss you now and say goodnight
But I'll still love you with all my might
I'll go to sleep and dream of you
Because I know your love is true.

Here in northern Minnesota we have a great variety of birds. Most kinds will migrate each year just like they do in other locals, some of them are hardy enough to remain her summer and winter. The larger birds like the Blue Jay and wood peckers can be real pests in my feeders as they like to spill many more seeds on the ground than what they eat. This attracts the deer in winter and the bears in summer. While I like to see them as well, I'd rather not have them around the yard because they are hard on our garden in summer, and the apple trees in winter. The little birds like the Gold Finches, the Red Polls, and the Chickadees are not nearly as messy and since I like to have them around, I keep several feeders around my yard filled with sunflower seeds all winter. These little birds will even come and knock on the windows if the feeders are empty. It is a bright spot in what might very well be a dreary winter. We consider that these little feathered friends are Gods promise that winter won't last forever.

Ode To A Chickadee

The Blue Jay is a beautiful bird,
At least, that is the words I've heard.
He's pretty, yes, I will agree,
But not as friendly as the chickadee.

With cap of black, and a vest of white,
This bird will cheer you when it comes in sight.
With feathers in various shades of gray,
This bird will brighten any day.

He always sings a happy song
Of "chick a dee, dee, dee," as he hops along.
They come to my feeder in early morn,
And that is how each day is born.

When sunflower seeds do fill the feeder,
I find their song is so much sweeter.
They'll even eat them from my hand
If I stand as still as I have planned.

They'll even sit upon my hat
Till around the house comes our old cat.
Then they all do fly away,
But I've just had a happy day.

Every writer I've ever known or talked to has told me that things will just be flowing and the words all seem to fall into place almost by themselves. Then the next time they sit down to write, it is like pulling teeth to get the words to flow. It isn't that they suddenly have lost their talent or any thing of that nature, it is just that they have reached a period of time when they are over come by something called writers block. It makes no difference what type of writing they specialize in, or how hard they try, they reach this period of time when the words just do not flow in a normal manner. I certainly am not immune to this malady and in fact I think I suffer from it on many occasions. This is something that I wrote one day to try to recover.

Writers Block

I try to create, I try to write,
From early morning, until late at night,
I try to put words on paper but then,
No words will flow from this old pen.

Try as I may, to write and create,
It's a jumble of words that don't sound great.
No words at all to make you sing
Just a lot of words that don't mean a thing.

My wife tries to help, she does her best,
Then it's up to me to do the rest.
I struggle and strive but the words are few,
Until I give up and say "I'm thru."

But I can't give up, it's not my way
When I still have so much to say.
I must write on, I've a story to tell,
Though I'm not telling it very well.

I carry on till the job is done,
But I can't say I've had much fun,
It's not my best, that much is true,
But think dear reader, it's all for you.

So tell me now what you would say,
If you had this kind of day.
Would you rant and rave and carry on,
Until at last the day is gone.

Would you try to work thru this curse,
Although you know each line is worse?
Would you pull your hair and say "That's it",
Or do like I did, and say "I Quit."

Sometimes I get up on my stump and tell the politicians what I think of them and their self serving ways. And it isn't only politicians that I despise, it's the people that feel that their wealth means everything should be their way, at the expense of others. Here in Minnesota we have an area along our northern border that is called the Boundary Waters Canoe Area Wilderness. That in conjunction with the Quetico Park, in Ontario comprise one of the largest road less areas that are within one days travel from cities such as the Twin Cities, Milwaukee, Chicago etc. that include millions of people. We have instituted laws and regulations to protect this area from development but each and every year there are politicians and land grabbers that try to get these rules relaxed so they can have their summer cabins in the area. This fight has been on going since the late nineteen fifties. Each year we seem to lose a few more acres.

Losing Our Wilderness

A beautiful lake that looks so serene,
From a hilltop above makes a beautiful scene.
The rocks and the trees that I see below
Will soon be covered over with snow

For this is late fall, and winter soon comes
To cover this land when the winter wind hums.
The ice will cover these waters so clear,
The bear will sleep, but not the wolf or the deer.

They'll run cross the ice in a race for their life
Cause the wolf's always hungry, and causes great strife.
This is the way, it's all natures plan
Of how life is beheld, if it's untouched by man

When man interferes the balance is gone
And nature can't sing its beautiful song.
The birds and the bears, their life they must change,
Because the ways of mankind, to them is so strange.

We put them on welfare until they become pests
Then we say, Well, lets get rid of the rest.
So we kill them all off, till we can't hear their song,
Then we look at each other and ask, What has gone wrong?

Mans interference, that's what has gone wrong.
No more will we hear nature's sweet song.
No more will we hear the loon on the lake
When all of the wilderness you insist you must take.

For this is a wilderness, surrounding these waters,
No houses or cabins with their sons and their daughters.
It has been decided, by big city folks,
That wilderness lovers are all stupid jokes.

A beautiful wilderness untouched and unspoiled.
But coming next year, this all will be soiled.
Allowed will be cabins with all their pollution
Because people in cities want this solution.

Some Indian once stood on the distant shore
And thought this would remain forever more.
I too once stood upon the shore
And prayed "God, keep it like this, I do implore"

But the word has come down from St. Paul town,
That this little wilderness will be torn down.
People may build their cabins there,
And gone will be the wolf and the bear.

There will be docks on the shore, and pollution in waters,
And lying on beaches, will be their sons and their daughters.
They'll drink as they dance, these wonderful fellers,
And tell of themselves, that they're still city dwellers.

They brag, and they brag, about all that they have
And how they will take it into their grave.
They drink, and they sing, with voices of glee,
Don't listen to reason, just listen to me.

I've got so much money, I could buy all this land,
So why shouldn't it be the way that I've planned?
The wolf and the bear are needed no more
Because now I'm here, and this is my shore.

My money and wealth say that I'm right,
And you, and your wilderness, are lost from my sight.
If this lake gets ruined, as well it may be,
St. Paul Politicians will get more for me.

I used to catch fish right here by the shore
But they'll soon be gone for ever more.
The jet ski's and skiers in their ridiculous race
Will quickly soon ruin this beautiful place.

I know I sound sad, and in fact I am bitter,
Because I've never been known as a quitter,
But my fire has gone out, and I'll fight no more,
To save this wilderness, and the beautiful shore.

St. Paul and Washington think they have a fix
To take lakes away from us country "hicks."
Sell it to those with money to spend
To buy politicians, till time has no end.

Some times I write things just to make you smile. This may not be considered to be humorous by some but it made me smile when I wrote it. Kentucky and Tennessee were both famous for the people that lived there, and the moonshine that was made up on the mountain. Though they may have neighbors who had lived alongside them for generations, but that never meant that they were friends. They would be treated as strangers if they were to trespass on some ones land where they were not invited.

Mountain Justice

There was a mountaineer
Whose given name was Fred.
His neighbor didn't like him,
So he pumped him full of lead.

He fell down from the mountain
And he landed on his head,
His wife came and got him,
And put him into bed.

She doctored him with moonshine,
Until his face was red,
And though she tried her very best,
By morning he was dead.

This "darlings" name was Mabel,
You might remember why,
When you read the coming story
Of where the bodies lie.

Now Mabel was a beauty.
As pretty as could be,
But she also had a temper,
As you will quickly see.

Now they had a grown up son there.
This fellows name was Jim,
Who went to see his neighbor,
Who did the same to him.

Mabel brought the body home
And laid him by his paw.
Then she told her neighbor,
I just became the law.

The neighbor laughed and danced about,
Then fell down to his knees,
When Mabel pulled her gun out,
And told that man to "freeze."

He started then to crawl away
So she shot him thru his hand,
To shoot him just a little
Was the way that Mabel planned.

Now the neighbor started talking,
About courting things and such,
But Mabel didn't listen,
Cause she didn't like him much.

Next she shot him thru the knees,
Just to hold him down.
This must have hurt a little,
Because it really made him frown.

You shot my man, you shot my son,
That really made me sad.
So now I'm here to shoot you
But not really very bad.

Just thru both feet and elbows,
And then the other hand.
And maybe once between the legs,
Is the way I've got it planned.

You'll live to tell the story
Of this awful, fateful day.
When pretty neighbor Mabel
Came, and made you pay.

Now this is mountain justice
Need I tell you more.
Don't mess with the men there,
The women even up the score.

CHAPTER TEN

One thing that over seventy years of living has taught me, sometimes painfully, is that all of the living creatures on this earth eventually die. Many times it is very painful when this happens. It is often painful to the creature that is dying, and often to others around it that seem to suffer just as much. This is true whether it be an animal, fish, tree or human.

I had a grove in my yard of a very large tree, with young trees growing around it. For unknown reasons the old tree began to die. In just a year it went from a strong tree that could handle any wind, to a withered bunch of branches that broke and fell from any breeze. Soon the whole tree lay on the ground. The younger trees around it also began to wither and die until it became just an ugly looking pile of brush that I cut down and burned. This taught me that there is life to most everything that is appreciated by others of its kind.

I've seen animals grieve when one of their friends or off spring died that was just as real as a human. I once had two dogs that I had raised from pups. They always did everything together. When they were eight years old one of the dogs made a mistake and ran into the road just as a car was passing. It was hit and killed right in front of the other dog. That dog spent the next several weeks lying in my front yard looking at the spot on the road where his pal had been killed. Yes, animals grieve just like humans do. I'm sure you've heard of many cases where a dog was left when his master died, and how they grieved for them.

The biggest difference that I can see between the grieving of other living beings, and humans is that we have the intelligence to know that all things must die to continue the road of life. We all must die to complete our journey that nature designed for us. Some lives are shorter, just as some are longer, than our own. Why this happens is a mystery to us all. Some people blame this on God but I believe they are wrong. We live by natures design only. God may have given us life, but then it was up to nature to control the where and when. To credit God with the happenings of our lives means we would have to blame God for the bad things that happen during our lives. I do not believe that God ever causes troubles and strife to something that he had created, just to see how they will act. My God is much too kind for that kind of thinking. For that reason I have no fear of dying. I know my time is limited, as is everyone's, but I think of death as my next grand adventure. For that reason I have written these last poems.

Every One Dies

Every one is sad when it's time to die,
But we can't change it if we try.
We can cry and carry on,
Until it's time for our final song.

We all must go, we have no choice.
Though loved ones complain, they have no voice.
We all must die, that's natures plan
Though doctors think it's in their hand.

Ministers too think they must try,
But all they give is an alibi,
Pray to God that we may live,
But that's one promise that God won't give.

All must die, we just wear out.
Though we contest it with a shout.
Science says, we know the way
To make you last another day.

Another day. Why that's absurd,
In fact, it's the silliest thing I've heard.
On the clock of infinity, our life's not a second
So one more day cannot be reckoned.

Another year is as a day.
It means nothing in this game we play.
So play the game as it's designed,
And when we're gone, be resigned.

We come, we go, we had our chance
To live our life, till the last dance.
We made our way, whether girl or lad,
And think of all the fun we had.

Though other folks have had more chances,
At luxury, fame, or romances,
That doesn't mean a better life,
Just more worries grief and strife.

They'll end up dead, just like you,
And have no more, that much is true.
Once we're dead we're all the same
And we return from whence we came.

So enjoy your life and forget me
Because I'm gone for eternity.
Enjoy your life, and all its ventures
Because dying, is your last adventure.

Will Anyone Remember Me?

When I lay me down to sleep
In that dark grave, cool and deep.
When my eyes are closed, and I cannot see,
For now I know you'll remember me.

I know at first on that fateful day,
When I at last have gone away,
Tears will be shed, they will run free,
And for today, you'll remember me.

Then when my grave is closed at last
And I am committed to the past,
No more to cry or to laugh with glee,
Who then will remember me?

And when the years have quickly flown,
And my name has now become unknown,
To all, except for two or three,
Will they alone remember me?

And when I'm lying in my bed,
Where grass is growing o'er my head,
When pain is gone, my soul set free,
Will anyone remember me?

When flesh and bones have met decay
And I am surely gone away,
Not even left is a memory.
Will there be anyone to remember me?

Then comes the day, when from on high
I'll hear the answer from the sky.
An answer to my humble plea,
Does anyone remember me?

Yes, I remember you this day,
And I remember where you lay.
I'll come for you, just wait and see,
You'll find I've not forgotten thee.

At last, an answer I have found,
While lying there beneath the ground.
My minds at ease, I'm worry free,
I know that God remembers me.

Now all of this is fine and dandy if you are looking forward to being consigned to a grave for eternity, but there are those of us that don't choose to follow this route. There are still people out there that think the style of burial that the Indians used may be the way to go. Hang them up in a tree and let the birds clean up the bones and then bury them. The sailors still occasionally bury their dead at sea. Then there is the other alternative which of course is cremation. I do believe that eventually cremation may become compulsory in some areas. There has been talk for some time about that method in the big cities around the country.

The Creamation Prayer

Don't bury me in the cold, cold ground,
It's always dark and there's no sound.
I want to hear the children play,
And feel the sunshine every day.

I want to see the geese each spring,
And hear the birds that always sing,
To hear the train as it rumbles by,
And see the airplanes in the sky.

I want to see the farmer's field,
And smell the crop, that it does yield,
To feel the rain, as it falls down,
Then makes its way across the ground.

To feel the change of every season,
Is all I need to give me reason,
To say, don't bury me in the ground.
I want to be able to look around.

Just put me in the burning fire,
Where in the smoke I'll fly much higher.
Then I'll fly around as so much dust,
And I'll be happy, in this I trust.

Scatter my ashes in a good stiff breeze
So I can drift up into the trees.
In flowers too, I'll make my home,
And on the bees I'll happily roam.

So many things to hear and see,
If you will do this thing for me.
I'll be out there without a care,
And you can find me, everywhere.

Eulogy

Now at last my time has come,
And I am now the chosen one.
The one to go, and find the way
On this my last and final day.

Don't cry for me or feel grief,
My life's been fun beyond belief.
I've no regrets to cry about
And I've missed nothing I can't do without.

Though I'll be lying neath the snow
I'll not be cold I'm sure you know.
I'll never hear the winters storm
Cause I'll be where it's safe and warm.

And summers heat won't bother me,
From all these things, I now am free.
The cares of man have passed me by.
So tell me now, why would I cry?

Cry for yourself to wash away
The grief you feel on this day.
To cleanse your thoughts, and clear your mind,
Since you again, have been left behind.

I leave you not for hurt or spite.
To punish you is not my right.
I leave you now because I must
Because we all are mortal dust.

A master plan is what we follow.
Any other plan would ring most hollow.
Our time on earth is but a span
And so we live as best we can.

Don't try to judge, or fix the blame.
It only adds to the hurting pain.
Accept what's come, and say goodbye
To those of us who had to die.

Your time will come, I know not when
And then perhaps we will meet again.
This is the way. I think its best,
So now loved ones, just let me rest.

The Guide

I met a man with smiling face,
On my last and final day.
He said "come with me, I'll be your guide,
And I'll show you the way."

Your life before is over now,
And you were sent to me,
To teach you of eternal life,
And of all the things you'll see.

I'll do my best to teach you well,
Of all that you must do,
To live in peace with those you love,
Be they many, or just a few.

This place we are, is not the same,
As those you've known before.
You've heard of milk and honey?
There's that, and so much more.

Here there is no worry.
Here there is no strife.
And here there is no end
To your eternal life.

You can live on here forever,
On that, you have my word.
Here in this lovely Eden,
That's provided by our Lord.

So take my hand
As we step inside,
Where your eyes will be
Opened wide.

You'll find friends
That you do know,
And lots of others,
That love you so.

What's that you say?
You don't like crowds?
Well, even here
Isolation is allowed.

Now, meet the man
That runs the show.
This one loves you
Don't you know?

So you do know that?
That's nice to see.
Because he loves you,
Eternally.

He nodded his head,
And I heard him say,
You're welcome here,
And you can stay.

So now I'm here
Where I will stay,
Because I knew
Jesus, is the way.

Edwards Brothers Malloy
Thorofare, NJ USA
August 16, 2013